"The ground was very rough and hard, and as we tore along, at an increasing pace that was very soon greater than any motorcar I had been in, I expected to be jerked and jolted. But the motion was wonderfully smooth - smoother yet - and then -! Suddenly there had come into it a new, indescribable quality - a lift - a lightness - a life! Very many there are now who know that feeling: that glorious, gliding sense that the seabird has known this million years, and which man so long and so vainly envied it, and which, even now, familiarity can never rob its charm. But picture if you can, what it meant for the first time; when all the world of Aviation was young and fresh and untried; when to rise at all was a glorious adventure, and to find oneself flying swiftly in the air, the too-good-to-be-true realization of a life-long dream. You wonderful aerial record breakers of today and of the years to come, whose exploits I may only marvel at and envy, I have experienced something that can never be yours and can never be taken away from me - the rapture, the glory and the glamour of "the very beginning."

Gertrude Bacon

(Writing of her flight with R.Sommer in August 1909.)

GLIDER BASICS
FROM FIRST FLIGHT TO SOLO

By

Thomas L Knauff

Other books by the author

After Solo

Glider Basics From Solo To License

Transition To Gliders

(A Glider Training Manual For Power Pilots)

Ridge Soaring The Bald Eagle Ridge

Accident Prevention Manual For Glider Pilots

Accident Prevention Manual For Glider Flight Instructors

Glider Flight Instructor Manual

The Bronze Badge Book

GLIDER BASICS
FROM FIRST FLIGHT TO SOLO

Cover Photo by George Vakkur

Drawings by James Taylor,

Malcolm Morrison

Charlie Weinert

Library of Congress Card Number 82-081473

ISBN 0-9605676-3-1

Published in USA by Knauff & Grove, Inc

Knauff & Grove, Inc.

3523 South Eagle Valley Rd

Julian, Pa 16844

www.eglider.org

ABOUT THE AUTHOR

Thomas Knauff is more than a writer; more than a flight instructor. He is one of the world's best soaring pilots. He is the first person to fly 750 and 1,000 kilometer triangles in the United States, and the first pilot to fly a 1,000 kilometer flight in a two-place glider in the United States. Tom holds the world record for a Goal and Return flight of 1,647 kilometers, the world's longest triangular flight of 1,362 kilometers, the World Free Distance record of 1,394 kilometers, and the first person to break the 200 kilometer per hour "barrier" with a 300 kilometer goal and return flight at 201.3 kph. He has also flown the second fastest 100 kilometer triangle in the world at 186 kph. Tom has set five world soaring records, and more than fifty US national records.

He is one of the premier flight instructors in the world. He has written numerous articles for Soaring Magazine, authored several books, and conducts many seminars and clinics that have improved the professionalism of all glider flight instructors and pilots. His instructional innovations include the TLAR pattern teaching methods included in this text. The FAA honored him as the Eastern Region Flight Instructor of the Year in 1997.

The soaring community needs a standardized training program that will ensure a well trained student. This alone will assure an improved safety record for our sport. Tom's books have become a rallying point for conscientious instructors and students.

Doris Grove

Doris Grove is the first woman to fly 1,000 kilometers in a glider, holds three world records, is a respected glider flight instructor, and a member of the Soaring Hall of Fame.

PREFACE

This book gives the student pilot and flight instructor the information needed to complete a pre-solo flight instruction course. Although I have tried to make sure all information is correct, no attempt was made to include every possible detail. Doing this would have required several volumes. It should be obvious to advanced pilots and instructors that, for clarity and simplicity, "the whole story" sometimes is not given.

The suggested pre-solo syllabus is a typical chain of events in one student's training program. However, the instructor often will find it necessary to deviate from this syllabus because of weather, equipment available, or the student's progress and previous lessons. Even the mood of the participants can, and should be, reason enough to deviate.

It is best to think of the syllabus in "phases." A student should not move to the next phase until the present phase is satisfactorily performed. In no case should a student solo until all required pre-solo maneuvers are performed with smoothness, accuracy and understanding.

Students must understand in aviation, a 70% is not a passing grade. In this sport, as in all of aviation, what you don't know can hurt you. Soaring instruction thus requires study and hard work, but it will reward you with satisfaction, fun, and the thrill of accomplishment. The rewards you will realize are not available in any other sport.

Comments about this manual should be addressed to me at Ridge Soaring Gliderport, Knauff & Grove Soaring Supplies, Julian, Pa 16844.

Good Luck,
Tom Knauff

TABLE OF CONTENTS

About the Author V

Preface vi

1. THE FLIGHT TRAINING PROGRAM ix

2. PRE SOLO SYLLABUS x

3. YOUR FIRST FLIGHT IN A GLIDER xiv

4. NOMENCLATURE 1

5. INSTRUMENTS 3

6. THE WING 7

7. THE PRIMARY FLIGHT CONTROLS 13

8. FLYING LESSON NUMBER ONE 25

9. WRITTEN TEST NUMBER ONE 28

10. STABILITY 31

11. WRITTEN TEST NUMBER TWO 38

12. FLIGHT NUMBER TWO 39

13. PRE-TAKEOFF CHECKLIST 43

14. SHALLOW, MEDIUM AND STEEP TURNS 45

15. WRITTEN TEST NUMBER THREE 49

16. GROUND HANDLING 50

17. PREFLIGHT 51

18. WRITTEN TEST NUMBER FOUR 54

19. SSA SIGNALS 56

20. AEROTOW TAKEOFF 57

21. AEROTOW 63

22. RUNNING THE WING 67

23. FORWARD STALLS 69

24. WRITTEN TEST NUMBER FIVE 76

25. TURNING STALLS 77

26. WRITTEN TEST NUMBER SIX 81

27. FLIGHT AT CRITICALLY SLOW SPEEDS 83

28. THERMALLING TECHNIQUE 85

29. SLACK ROPE 89

30. PATTERN ENTRY 91

31. LANDINGS (TLAR) 97

32. WRITTEN TEST NUMBER SEVEN 117

33. PREMATURE TERMINATIONS OF THE TOW 119

34. SLIPS 127

35. CROSSWIND LANDINGS 131

36. STEEP TURNS 133

36. GROUND REFERENCE MANEUVERS 135

37. SOLO! 141

38. ABC AND BRONZE BADGES 143

39. FAI SOARING AWARDS 146

40. TEST ANSWERS 148

BASIC GLOSSARY OF AVIATION TERMINOLOGY 155

BIBLIOGRAPHY 162

THE COST OF FLYING GLIDERS 163

INDEX 164

WRITTEN TESTS

#1 28

#2 STABILITY 38

#3 SHALLOW, MEDIUM AND STEEP TURNS 49

#4 PREFLIGHT 54

#5 FORWARD STALLS 76

#6 TURNING STALLS 87

#7 TLAR 117

WRITTEN TEST ANSWERS

#1 148

#2 STABILITY 149

#3 SHALLOW, MEDIUM AND STEEP TURNS 149

#4 PREFLIGHT 150

#5 FORWARD STALLS 151

#6 TURNING STALLS 152

#7 TLAR 153

THE FLIGHT TRAINING PROGRAM

Welcome to what may be the most exciting, rewarding sport of all — soaring! You are embarking on a learning experience that will be a never-ending quest to make yourself a better, safer pilot.

Most people can complete the requirements for solo flight in 25 to 30 flights, provided they fly regularly. It is common for people to take the solo training during a week to ten day period at a commercial glider school or soaring club that offer every day services. Many clubs, however, operate only on weekends. Learning to fly only on weekends will typically take several more flights. Earning the private glider license will usually take a few months, but some people who take a concentrated course can finish in only a couple of weeks.

Another not-so-inaccurate method to estimate how many flights it will take to solo is to figure one flight for each year old you are. It's not so much that older people take longer to learn as it is that younger people take less time. It is common for some people to require twice the average number of training flights to solo. These same people often become expert soaring pilots.

If you find it is necessary to take lessons on an occasional basis, it is important to plan to take many flights as close together as possible as you approach the time to solo.

Learning to soar requires no technical background or training, but you will have to learn to control the glider in a new three-dimensional world. This is not difficult to do, but requires a thorough understanding of a new environment. With practice and your instructor's guidance, you will develop the ability to soar, just as thousands of others have.

At the beginning of your flight training, you will be issued a Student Pilot Certificate. The only requirement for this certificate is that you are able to state that you have no known physical disability that would make you unable to pilot a glider. If there is any question as to your physical health or abilities, you may be required to visit a flight surgeon for an opinion. Physically handicapped people often are able to obtain glider licenses.

After earning your private glider license, you will most likely continue your training in advance soaring techniques. Indeed you should.

Sound like a lot of work? It is, and it isn't. Your training will consist of reading several texts, ground instruction, flight instruction and finally, solo practice. You will take a written test administered by the Federal Aviation Agency and then a flight test by an examiner when you have fulfilled all other requirements.

The rate you proceed, and the cost to learn to fly will depend greatly on your commitment to the learning process. It is important for you to read, and commit to memory all of this and other texts. In aviation, a 70%, 80% or 90% is not a passing grade, because what you don't know can hurt you! Your instructor will not only demand that you know the correct answers to questions, but you will also be required to answer those questions in a very specific manner. If you are unable to respond with correct answers, the instructor is obligated to cover the information in a costly classroom discussion. The end of chapter tests in this book will help you respond to some of the important questions.

The glider training you receive is excellent background if you plan to continue on to your power license. It has become recognized that glider pilots make the best candidates for a power license.

PRE SOLO SYLLABUS

Phase I

Flight 1. Controls and their functions — the wing, angle of attack, shallow turns, speed control, use of the trim, aileron drag, yaw string.

Flight 2. Stability — roll, pitch, and yaw, more turning practice, cockpit check list, collision avoidance.

Phase II

Flight 3. Aerotow, shallow, medium, steep turns, ground handling, attempted landing while instructor talks student down and operates dive brakes.

Flight 4. Flight at minimum controllable airspeed, imminent forward stalls, reduced G.

Flight 5. Preflight, aerotow, forward stalls, turns, turns, turns.

Phase III

Flight 6. TLAR demonstration, takeoff, say 200 feet.

Flight 7 - 10. TLAR, aerotow, thermalling, pattern entry.

Flight 11. Turning stalls (imminent and full stalls).

Flight 12. Basic weight and balance, flight manual, wake turbulence, signals, turning stalls.

Phase IV

Flight 13 - 18. Aerotow, 360's, 720's, stalls, TLAR, right hand pattern, slack in towrope, ground reference maneuvers, equipment malfunctions.

Flight 19. Forward rope break - unassisted takeoff.

Flight 20. 200' rope break - downwind landing.

Flight 21. 200' rope break.

Phase V

Flight 22 - 24. Pattern flights, slips, crosswind landings, high drag configurations.

Pre-solo written test.

Flight 25. Solo.

PRIVATE GLIDER PILOT SYLLABUS

The following are the knowledge and skill requirements specified by the FAA for a private glider rating. Some items are knowledge requirements taught during a ground school or home study course. Other items are skill requirements taught during flight training. Some are combinations of skill and knowledge. Starred items (*) are minimum solo requirements. Student cross country requirements are marked with a (@). Some soaring sites may require additional minimum solo items because of airspace restrictions, unique soaring conditions, cross winds etc. Refer to FARs and Practical Test Standards for complete requirements. Motorglider requirements are excluded.

_____ 1. FAR Part 1, 43, 61, 91, and 830.

__a. Eligibility requirements. __b. *Medical requirements. __c. *Personal logbook. __d. FCC station license. __e. Glider pilot certificates; privileges, and limitations. __f. Glider and tow pilot recency of experience requirements. __g. * Airworthiness and registration certificates. __h. * Maintenance requirements and records. __i. * General operating rules. __j. * Flight rules. __k. Accident reporting.

___ 2. Glider Flight Manual.

__a. * Flight characteristics, Operating limitations, equipment list. __b. * Performance charts, tables and data.   __c. * Weight and balance. __d. * Ballast and it's effect on performance.

___3. * Glider Assembly, and Disassembly.

___4. Flight Preparation and Planning.

__a. * National airspace system. __b. * Controlled airspace. __c. * Special use airspace. __d. Enroute checkpoints. __e. Go ahead points. __f. Using lift sources and speed between lift sources. __g. Terrain considerations. __h. Selecting landing areas. __i. Aeronautical Information Manual. __j. @ Navigation, aeronautical charts. __k. Cross country emergency procedures. __l. VFR navigation/pilotage, dead reckoning. __m. FAA advisory circulars.

___5. Personal Equipment.

__a. High altitude. __b. Varying terrain. __c. Long distances. __d. Climatic conditions. __e. Oxygen systems. __f. Parachutes.

___6. Flight Instruments and Associated Aircraft Systems.

__a. *Magnetic compass. __b. * Yaw string. __c. * Airspeed indicator. __d. * Altimeter. __e. * Variometer. __f. Inclinometer. __g. Total energy compensator. __h. Gyroscopic instruments __ i. Electrical system __j. *Landing gear. __ k. @ Avionics

___7. Soaring Weather.

__a. * Recognition of critical weather situations and conditions suitable for soaring flight.

__b. * Basic VFR weather minimums. __c. @ Adverse weather conditions.

___8. Pilot Weather Reports and Forecasts.

__a. @ Procurement and use of aeronautical weather reports & forecasts. __b. Area and terminal forecasts. __c. Winds & temperatures aloft. __d. Severe weather watch bulletin. __e. Surface analysis chart. __f. Weather depiction chart. __g. Radar summary chart. __h. Composite moisture stability chart. __i. Significant weather prognosis. __j. Effect of density altitude and wind on performance. __k. Severe weather outlook chart. __l. SIGMET's and AIRMET's. __m. NOTAM's. __n. PIREP's. __o. Wind shear reports __p. @ Estimating visibility. __q. Making sound go-no-go decisions based on weather.

___9. Stability Charts.

__a. Pressure and temperature lapse rates. __b. Atmospheric instability. __c. Thermal index. __d. Thermal production. __e. Cloud formation and identification. __f. Frontal weather. __g. Other lift sources.

___10. Hazards Associated With Thunderstorms.

___11. Preflight.

__a. * Line inspections. __b. * Tie down. Control lock and wheel chock removal. __c. * Ice and frost removal. __ d. *Written checklists __e. *Flight control __f. *Proper assembly __g. * Personal equipment. __h. * Tow rope, weak links, towline inspection, releases. __i. * Launch equipment inspection - tow hitches, releases. __j. * Structural damage. __k. * Noting discrepancies. __l. * Ground handling. __m. Postflight procedures.

__12. Launches, Aerotow and/or Ground tows. *Surface operations.

a. *Pre-takeoff checklists. __b. *Takeoff. __c. *Aerotow, including airspeeds. __*High or low tows. __e.*Signals. __f.*Safety precautions. __g. *Release procedures. __h. *Slack towline procedures.__i. Boxing the wake. __j.*Wake turbulence. __k. Windshear. __l. Density altitude.

___13. Aerotow, Abnormal Procedures.

__a. * Tow plane power loss during takeoff. __b. * Tow plane power failure at altitude. __c. * Glider release failure. __d. * Towline break during takeoff. __e. * Glider and tow plane release failure. __f. * Porpoising.

___14. Precision Maneuvering.

__a. * Straight glides. __b. * Turns, Shallow, medium, steep turns. __c. * Flight at minimum controllable airspeed. __d. * Imminent forward and turning stalls. __e. * Full stalls, forward stalls. __f. * Spirals. __g. Spin entry, spins, spin recovery technique. __h. * Collision avoidance. __i. Turns to headings. __ j. *Descents with and without drag devices.

___15. Critical Performance Speeds.

__a. * Never exceed speed. __b. * Minimum sink speed. __c. * Maneuvering speed.

__d. * Rough air redline. __e. * Speed to fly. __f. * Best glide speed.

___16. Traffic Patterns.

__a. *Entry and departure procedures __b. * Co-existing traffic patterns. __c. * Rules.

__d. * Pre-landing checklist. __e. *Collision avoidance. __f. *Wake turbulence

___17. Normal Landings.

__a. * Use of dive brakes, spoilers, and flaps. __b. * Accuracy approaches and landings.

__c. * Faulty approaches. __d. *Side slips, forward slips, turning slips.

___18. *Crosswind Takeoffs and Landings.

___19. Downwind Landings.

___20. *Ground Reference Maneuvers.

___21. @ Off Field Landings (simulated).

___22. Emergency Procedures, and Equipment Malfunctions.

___23. Aeronatical decision making & Judgment.

___24. Soaring Techniques. __a. *Thermal Soaring. __b. *Ridge and slope soaring.
__c. Wave soaring. __d. Mountain soaring. __ e. *Convergence lift

___25. Recovery From Unusual Attitudes.

__a. High speed spirals. __b. Excessive bank angles. __c. Excessive pitch angles. __d. Crossed
control stalls. __e. High sink rates.

___26. Medical Factors.

___27. @ Cross Country Emergency Conditions and Terrain problems.

___28. Flight Test. __a. Fight test requirements. __b. Written test requirements.

__c. Use of distractions during flight test.

ADDITIONAL FLIGHT MANEUVERS

__*Control functions __*Yaw string __*Use of trim __*Aileron drag __Flap usage __Spins
__Benign spiral mode __*Low "G" maneuvers __Unassisted takeoffs __Left and right hand
landing patterns __Accuracy landings __*Wheel brake __*Rope breaks, land straight
ahead __*Rope breaks above 200 feet. __*No instrument flight __Radio procedures
__*Student training area

April, 2,000

YOUR FIRST FLIGHT IN A GLIDER

Prospective students usually want to take a flight on their very first visit to the gliderport. It would be best, of course, to read about some of the basics so you can better understand what happens during your first lesson. But, we understand your impatience to see what soaring is like, so let's go!

The instructor will show you how to arrange the seat belts before you get in to allow room to sit down. When you get in, try not to step on the upholstery, and be careful not to grab onto anything fragile. You will be shown where to pull, push, hold on, and where you can't without damaging the glider.

Step all the way into the cockpit and sit down. The seat belts are a little complicated; you will need some help in fastening them the first time or two. It is important to be sure the seat belts are snug so you don't 'float' around if you should encounter bumps during the flight. Your instructor will give you a tour around the cockpit, and allow time to become accustomed to your new surroundings.

The instructor will do most of the flying on this 'orientation' flight. You might notice how little the instructor needs to move the controls during the flight. You will be allowed to control the glider for a few moments if you like. Listen for the difference in sound as the glider changes airspeed. Do not spend too much time looking at the glider's instruments. Look outside as much as possible and enjoy the view.

All too soon, the flight will end as the instructor makes a smooth landing. Feel free to ask questions during and after the flight. The instructor may suggest you do some reading before answering some of your questions.

Your flight training records are recorded in a *Glider Pilot's Logbook*. An accurate record of your flight training is essential to obtain a license, and to document experience requirements.

This record of your flying history will become a personally valuable document. You may keep notes of particularly interesting flights, badges, records, contests, and even staple barograph traces and photographs which you will treasure. Take time to neatly record the facts of your flights.

BASIC NOMENCLATURE

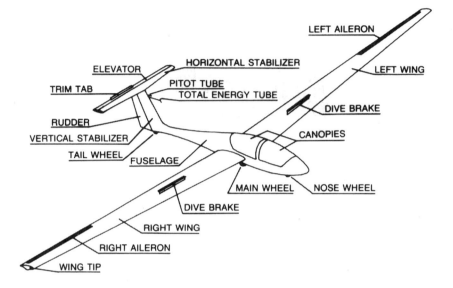

GLIDER OR SAILPLANE?

The difference between a glider and a sailplane used to be that a glider's performance was so poor it would only descend after being launched. It's performance would not permit it to remain aloft, using available lift in the atmosphere, or soar. A sailplane's performance is better than a glider, and this fact is proven by its ability to stay aloft and *soar*.

We now know much more about the forces available in nature, and it is possible to make the poorest performing gliders soar. In fact, all modern gliders are sailplanes. The term 'gliders' or 'sailplanes' is now used interchangeably by sailplane pilots. (Or is it "glider pilots?") Brake Control

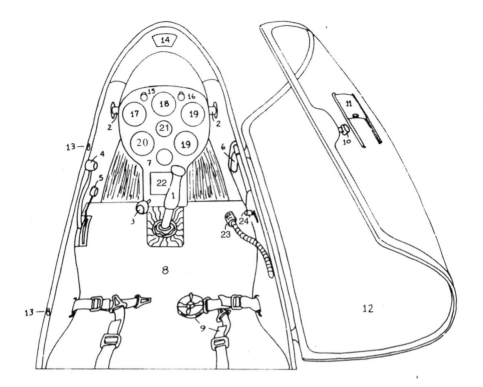

1. Control Stick
2. Rudder Pedals
3. Tow Release Knob*
4. Dive Brake Control
5. Trim Control
6. Landing Gear Retraction Handle
7. Instrument Panel
8. Pilot's Seat
9. Quick Release Seat Belt/Shoulder Harness
10. Canopy Locking Lever
11. Sliding Vent Window
12. Canopy

13. Canopy Locking Pins
14. Air Vent
15. Air Vent Control
16. Rudder Pedal Adjustment Knob
17. Altimeter
18. Airspeed Indicator
19. Variometers
20. Final Glide Computer
21. Compass
22. Radio
23. Microphone
24. Canopy Jettison Knob

*Note: Red in Schweizer sailplanes, Yellow in most other sailplanes.

THREE BASIC INSTRUMENTS

ALTIMETER

The altimeter shows the altitude of the aircraft by measuring air pressure. It is basically a barometer, but instead of showing barometric pressure, it is calibrated in feet. Since the daily barometric pressure changes, it has an adjustment knob so an adjustment can be made to account for the barometric pressure at the moment.

Regulations requires the altimeter be set to field elevation above sea level. (MSL or "Mean Sea Level.") In flight, the altimeter will indicatethe height above sea level. During flight, to figure the height of the glider above ground (AGL or "Above Ground Level.") , subtract the ground elevation from the indicated altitude. Example: Indicated altitude 2,500 feet MSL, less 800 feet ground elevation, equals 1,700 feet AGL.

The interior of a glider in flight is usually at a slightly lower pressure than the outside of the aircraft, and some altimeters are vented only to the cockpit pressure. This results in an insignificant erroneous reading . A more accurate altimeter will be vented to a static vent on the aircraft.

AIRSPEED INDICATOR

The airspeed indicator is a very sensitive instrument which measures the differential pressure between pitot, or impact pressure, and static pressure. (You feel impact pressure when you stick your hand out the window of a moving car.) It indicates the airspeed at which the glider is moving through the air (not the speed along the ground.) The instrument can be calibrated in several different speed indications. Knots, miles per hour, and kilometers per hour are the most common. Knots are convenient because aeronautical charts are marked in degrees and seconds, (one second is approximately one nautical mile). If you also have the variometer in knots, you can simply divide airspeed, in knots, by your rate of sink, in knots, to determine the L/D, or glide ratio of the glider at that moment.

The airspeed indicator has several colored markings:

The white sector is the speed flaps may be used.
The green sector is the normal operating range.
The yellow sector is permitted only in calm air.
The red line is the never-exceed speed.

Some airspeed indicators have a small yellow triangle at the minimum recommended landing pattern airspeed. (Add 1/2 of any wind to this speed plus a factor for turbulence or gusts).This usually also corresponds to the glider's maximum L/D speed in calm air.

Knots   MPH   Kmh

10 kts = 11.5 mph   18.5 Kmh
20 Kts = 23 mph   37 Kmh
40 KTS = 46 mph   74 Kmh
50 Kts = 57.5 mph   92 Kmh
→ 60 KTS = 69 mph   110 km.
70 KTS = 80.5 Mph
→ 80 KTS = 90 mph   148 Kmh
90 KTS = 103.6 mph
→ 100 KTS = 115 Mph   185 Km
110 KTS = 126.6 mph
120 KTS = 138 mph
→ 130 KTS = 150 mph   241 Kmh

100%   +15%   +85%

VARIOMETER

The variometer is essential for modern soaring flight. It is a very sensitive instrument showing if the glider is climbing or descending, and how fast. The variometer can be calibrated in knots, feet per minute, or meters per second.

Basic variometers work by detecting a rate of airflow between a capacity and a static source.

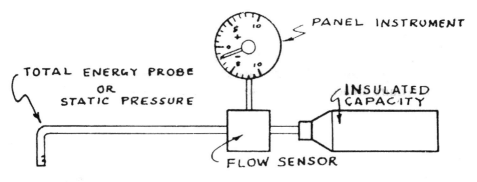

When the glider climbs, the air inside the capacity expands and flows out through the instrument; when the glider descends, the air reverses flow into the flask. The rate at which this air flow causes the needle to deflect the indicated amount.

Electric variometers work on the principle of air flowing past thermistors causing differential cooling, which requires differential voltage to keep the thermistors at a constant temperature. Electric variometers tend to be much quicker than mechanical variometers, with a 1 1/2 second delay being average, whereas a mechanical variometers typically have double that or even worse.

TOTAL ENERGY

A variometer installed as described will work just fine, showing when the glider climbs and descends. The problem with this simple system is when the pilot pulls the control stick back, the variometer will show the resulting temporary climb. These pilot-induced climbs and descents are commonly called "stick thermals." These stick thermals can be cancelled out by installing any one of several total energy devices. The most common of these is a total energy probe. A total energy probe is usually a bent tube with slots or tiny holes on the downstream side, mounted on the leading edge of the vertical stabilizer.

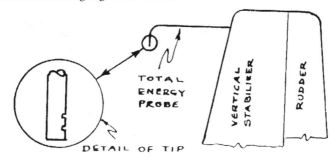

There are other ways to produce total energy, but the T.E. probe is simple, effective and inexpensive. Electric variometers can perform this task electronically, but require an accurate static source, which may not be available on the aircraft.

An important option is an audio device for the variometer. This can be installed on either a mechanical variometer or an electric one. The audio provides an audible sound when the variometer needle deflects. The typical climb tone is a broken beep-beep-beep that increases in pitch and frequency as the climb rate improves. The descending sound is a steady tone decreasing in pitch as the sink rate increases.

The variometer should be equipped with a speed-to-fly ring. More on that in another chapter.

Competition pilots will often equip their gliders with the newest electronic gadgetry. Audio speed-to-fly directors and flight computers are very useful to reduce the mental workload so the pilot can concentrate on tactics, flying accurately, collision avoidance and where to fly next in search of the best lift.

THE WING

The wing, passing through the air, produces a force called *lift*. This lift is what makes the flight of all aircraft possible. In the case of a glider, the lift produced by the wing permits the glider to come down through the air at a very slow rate and glide great distances. A typical modern sailplane might have a *sink rate* of less than two feet per second and a *glide ratio* of more than 40 to 1 in still air. Starting one mile above the earth, it could glide a distance of more than 40 miles. Very high performance gliders have a maximum glide ratio over 60 to 1!

HOW THE WING PRODUCES LIFT

A wing has a cross section shape called an *airfoil*. The wing of a typical training glider is flat on the bottom and curved on the top. There are many different airfoil shapes.

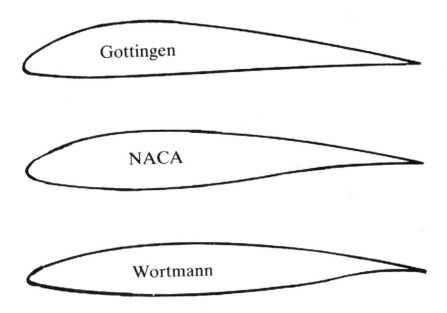

Gottingen

NACA

Wortmann

Common Airfoil Shapes

As the aircraft moves through the air, an equal and opposite airflow is created. This airflow is called *relative airflow*, or sometimes, *relative wind*.

To understand relative airflow, it is helpful to picture an automobile traveling along the highway. If the driver holds a hand out the window, a strong relative airflow would be felt coming from opposite the direction of the car's travel.

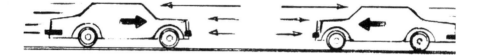

A glider's travel through the air is forward and downward, because gravity is pulling the glider down. The relative airflow is therefore from the area in front of, and below the wing.

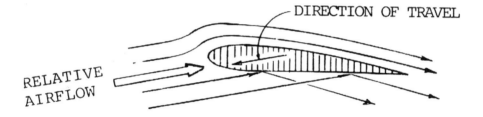

The air compresses along the bottom of the wing, creating a positive pressure. This positive pressure accounts for about 20% of the lift produced. The air flowing over the top of the wing is forced to speed up, which causes the air to thin out slightly. This causes a suction (reduced pressure) that pulls up on the top of the wing. The reduced pressure produces the greater part of the total lift produced by the wing.

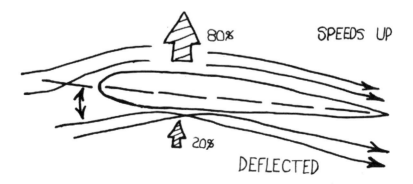

The airfoil shape of the wing also causes the airflow to be deflected downward. One of Sir Isaac Newton's laws states, "For every action, there is an equal and opposite reaction." The equal and opposite reaction of the wing forcing the air down, is for the air to force the wing upward.

The combination of unequal air pressures and deflected airflow create an opposite upward force producing lift.

ANGLE OF ATTACK

As noted before, the relative airflow meets the bottom of the wing from the area in front of and below the wing.

The angle the relative airflow meets the wing is called *Angle of Attack.*

The amount of lift the wing produces depends upon the speed of the relative airflow (the faster the airflow, the greater the lift), and also the angle of attack (the higher the angle of attack, the greater the lift.)

If you increase the angle of attack of the wing, the air strikes the bottom at a more direct angle and is also forced to travel even faster over the top. This creates additional compression, suction, and deflected airflow which creates more lift.

The airflow must flow smoothly over the surface. If the angle of attack is too high, the airflow breaks away from the top surface in turbulent airflow. This is called a *stall*. More on this later.

IT IS IMPORTANT TO REMEMBER THE FOLLOWING:

INCREASING THE ANGLE OF ATTACK, INCREASES LIFT.

DECREASING THE ANGLE OF ATTACK, DECREASES LIFT.

When the angle of attack changes, two other things change. First, is the change in the *lift* produced as mentioned above. Second, the amount of *drag* produced by the wing is also changed.

You can demonstrate this by holding your hand out a car window while driving.

Holding your hand at a low angle of attack, you will feel little resistance, or drag.

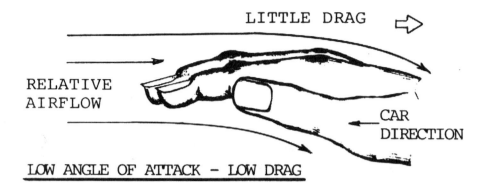

The third change occurring when angle of attack is changed, is the airspeed changes. Imagine coasting down a hill on a bicycle. If you lean over, presenting a small profile, (low angle of attack) the bike coasts fast. When you sit up, (high angle of attack) you present more surface to the relative airflow (creating more drag) and the bike slows down.

Tilting your hand upward, you increase the angle of attack. You will feel an increase in both lift and drag.

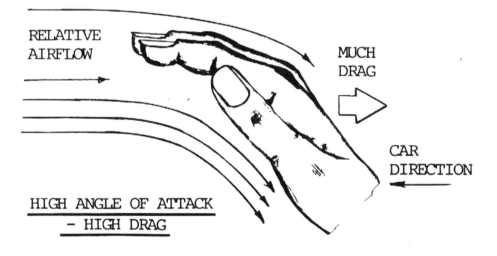

This has been an explanation of how a wing works. You must completely understand the relationship between the wing, relative airflow, and angle of attack.

The words "angle of attack" and the relationships of lift, drag and speed will be very important throughout your flight training.

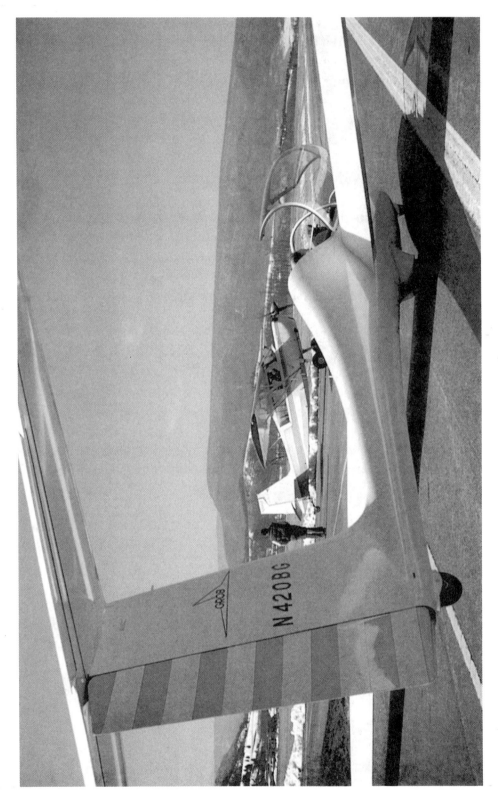

THE PRIMARY FLIGHT CONTROLS

Most gliders have several controls — flaps, spoilers, dive brake, release, trimmer. However, three controls are essential to controlled flight: the *elevator*, *ailerons* and the *rudder*. These three controls are commonly called, the *primary flight controls*.

The elevator is moved by a fore and aft movement of the control stick, the ailerons by a sideways movement of the same control stick, and the rudder is moved with the pilot's feet on the rudder pedals.

In a glider, the control stick is always held in the right hand, because other controls will be used at times with the left hand.

When flying, the aircraft balances on a single point called the *Center of Gravity*, or "C.G." Each of the primary flight controls cause the aircraft to rotate about the C.G.

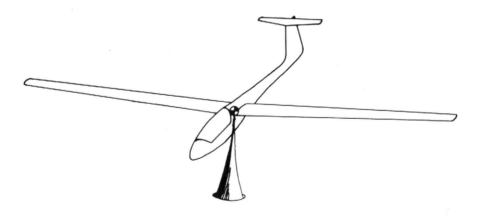

THE ELEVATOR

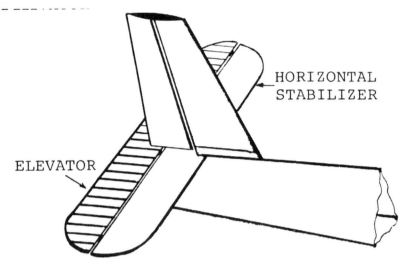

HORIZONTAL
STABILIZER

ELEVATOR

Uninformed people naturally believe the elevator makes an aircraft go up and down. That's not true.

Really important!

THE ELEVATOR'S ONLY FUNCTION IS TO CONTROL
THE ANGLE OF ATTACK OF THE WING.

The elevator is a horizontal airfoil hinged to the horizontal stabilizer on the tail of the glider. Moving the elevator up or down with a backward or forward movement of the control stick in the cockpit, changes the flat, streamlined airfoil into a curved one. This creates an upward or downward force which moves the tail of the glider up or down, pitching the nose of the fuselage up and down, thus changing the angle of attack of the wing.

Moving the elevator down, by moving the control stick forward, creates an airfoil which lifts the tail, lowers the nose, and reduces the angle of attack of the wing. In this case, the glider's nose *pitches* down about the center of gravity.

Remember, when the angle of attack changes, three things change — lift, drag, and speed. It's not likely a pilot will notice the change in lift or drag. An aircraft does not have, or need a "lift meter" nor a "drag meter". But two things easily noticed when the elevator is moved, changing the angle of attack of the wing, is the nose of the glider moves to a different "pitch attitude" relative to the horizon, and a definite change in airspeed occurs. When the control stick is moved forward, the elevator moves down causing the tail to rise, and the nose of the glider to pitch nose down. The wing flies at a reduced angle of attack. This causes a reduction in drag, and the glider speeds up. You can see the change in pitch attitude and hear the change in airspeed.

Airspeed is controlled by controlling the angle of attack of the wing with the elevator! Remember this.

14

A WORD ABOUT UP AND DOWN

The elevator can cause a glider to momentarily gain altitude if the glider's initial speed is above stall speed. Suppose a glider is traveling at 90 miles per hour and the pilot pulls the stick back. The angle of attack will be increased so that the lift *potential* is increased. The word 'potential' is necessary because when we increase the angle of attack, we also increase drag (which decreases speed). Since the amount of lift the wing generates is a function of both angle of attack and the speed of the relative airflow, the lift will first increase, causing the glider to climb.

Then the lift will begin to decrease as the speed begins to slow. The wing will produce less and less lift as the speed decreases. The glider will climb less and less, then begin to sink again. It may even stall and drop it's nose. (More on stalls later.)

A glider can change excess height into airspeed, and excess airspeed into height, within limitations. A glider can dive, accelerate to a high airspeed and then climb briefly until the airspeed stabilizes.

It's kind of like a bicycle coasting fast down one hill, and, with a high speed at the bottom, coast part way up the next hill until the extra energy dissipates.

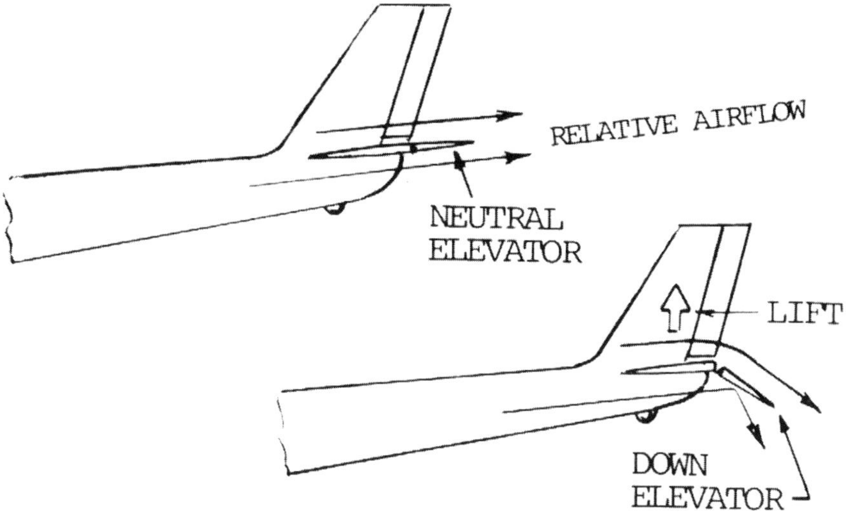

RELATIVE AIRFLOW

NEUTRAL ELEVATOR

LIFT

DOWN ELEVATOR

THE AILERONS

The ailerons are on the trailing, or aft edge, of the wing near the wing tips. They are controlled by moving the control stick sideways. They are connected together so when one aileron goes down, the other one goes up.

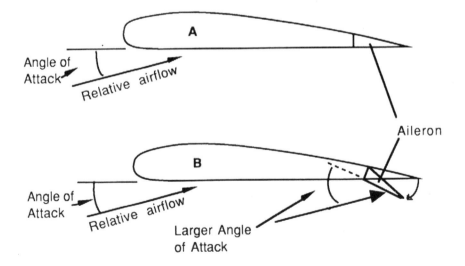

To understand how an aileron works, it is necessary to take another look at airfoils and angle of attack.

The relative airflow appears to strike both of the above airfoils in the same manner. But notice how the deflected aileron creates an extra curve on the bottom surface of airfoil B. This causes the relative airflow to strike at different angles of attack at the different points. If we measure the angle of attack at all points along the bottom of the airfoil and then averaged them, we would find the average angle of attack of airfoil B is higher than airfoil A. Airfoil B therefore has a higher angle of attack and produces more lift.

Moving the aileron down changes the shape of the airfoil causing that portion of the wing to increase it's angle of attack and produce more lift.

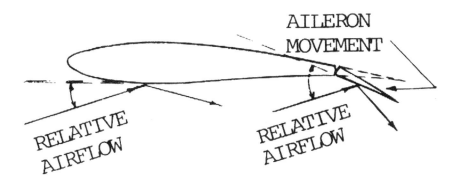

The aileron on the opposite wing moves the opposite way, (up), causing that portion of the wing to produce less lift.

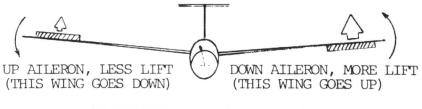

UP AILERON, LESS LIFT
(THIS WING GOES DOWN)

DOWN AILERON, MORE LIFT
(THIS WING GOES UP)

(FRONT VIEW, IT'S COMIN' AT YOU)

Moving the control stick to the pilot's right moves the left aileron down, and the right aileron up. The net result is an unbalanced lifting force which causes the glider to roll or bank. In the case of the above drawing, the glider banks to the glider's right.

WHY WE WANT TO CONTROL THE ANGLE OF BANK

The lift that is produced by the wing is always perpendicular to the wing.

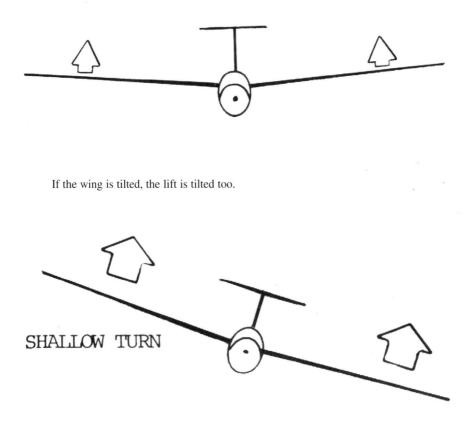

If the wing is tilted, the lift is tilted too.

SHALLOW TURN

The force produced by the wing is now lifting to the side. This causes the glider to turn. The glider is 'lifted' around the turn by the lift produced by the wing being tilted to one side.

If we take a simple paper airplane, or a Frisbee disc, which has NO controls whatever, and throw it level, it will fly straight until something upsets the balance. If we throw the same paper glider or disc with the wings tilted or banked, it will turn. Fold up a paper glider and try it.

It is very important to understand there is NO control which turns the glider. Lift, produced by the wing, and tilted to the side, lifts the glider through a turn.

RATE OF TURN

Rate of turn is how quickly the glider changes direction. The rate of turn is determined by the bank angle. A shallow bank angle will cause a slow rate of turn and it will take a longer time to turn through an arc. A steep bank angle will cause a rapid rate of turn. (Airspeed also affects rate of turn.)

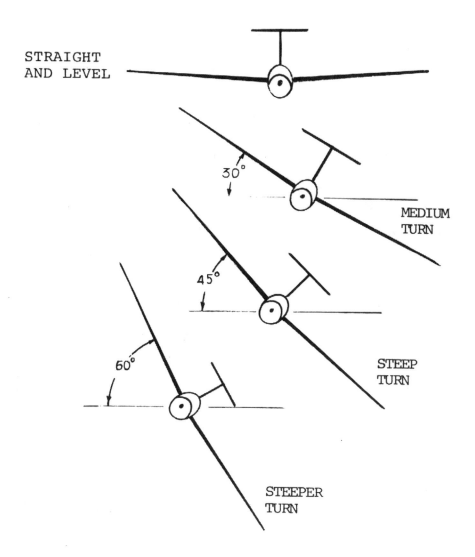

STRAIGHT
AND LEVEL

30°

MEDIUM
TURN

45°

STEEP
TURN

60°

STEEPER
TURN

SUMMARY

The wing produces lift.

The ailerons control bank angle.

The glider is lifted around a turn.

THE RUDDER

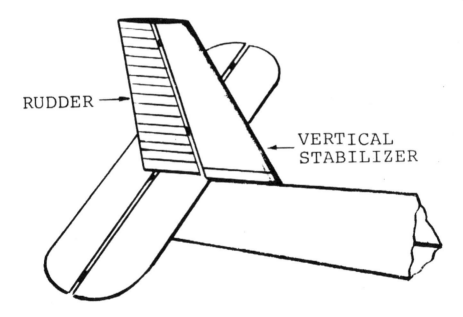

RUDDER

VERTICAL
STABILIZER

The rudder is the least understood control on the glider. It is estimated that 70% of all pilots don't fully understand why an aircraft has a rudder!

To understand the rudder, we must take another look at the ailerons.

As explained earlier, moving an aileron down causes that portion of the wing to have an increased angle of attack.

Increasing the angle of attack causes more lift, which raises that wing. But, anytime you increase angle of attack, you also increase drag, which reduces speed.

For every action there is an equal and opposite reaction. When we move the aileron down we get a desired result — an increase in lift. But we also get an undesired reaction — increased drag. And with drag comes a decrease in airspeed.

In the following example the pilot wants the glider to bank to the right so the glider will then turn right. When the control stick is moved to the right, the left aileron goes down and creates more lift to raise the left wing. At the same time, however, this lowered aileron causes an undesirable increase in drag which slows the left wing down and causes the glider to yaw, or veer, to the left — the opposite direction of our intended turn.

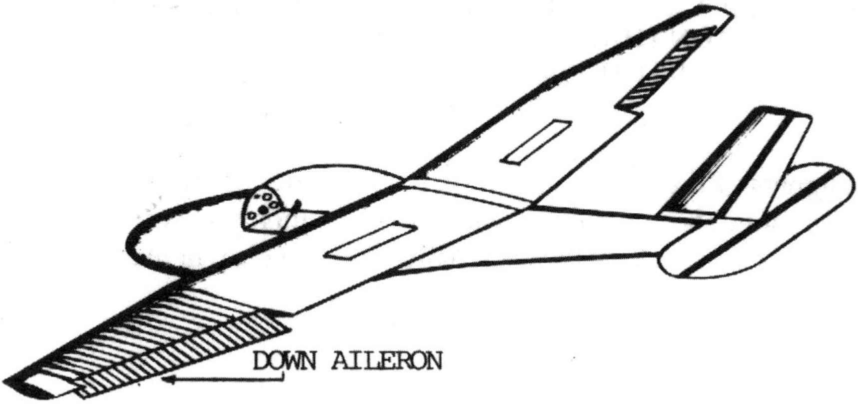

DOWN AILERON

INCREASED ANGLE OF ATTACK
OVER SHADED PORTION OF WING

This undesirable response is called *aileron drag*, or sometimes, *adverse yaw*.

THE RUDDER IS USED TO

COUNTERACT AILERON DRAG.

The pilot controls the rudder with foot operated rudder pedals (see item #2, page 2.) Pressing the left rudder pedal causes the rudder to deflect to the left which forces the tail to the right, causing the nose of the glider to *yaw* to the left.

Your instructor will demonstrate aileron drag and show you how the glider reacts both with and without proper rudder usage.

When the ailerons are moved, aileron drag tries to swing the nose of the glider opposite the desired direction of the turn. This causes the glider to skid sideways through the air, causing unwanted drag. A proper amount of rudder will counteract this undesirable effect.

When a pilot moves the ailerons, the rudder pedals must be moved at the same time. If the control stick is moved to the right, the right rudder pedal must pressed.

In order to make a proper, coordinated turn, (say to the right) the pilot will move the control stick to the right, and, at the same time, move the right rudder pedal approximately the same amount to overcome the aileron drag. Once the glider assumes the desired bank angle, both the aileron and rudder are returned to approximately the neutral position. It is a common fault of new pilots to want to continue using excessive rudder as long as they are turning.

RIGHT AILERON MOVES UP DECREASING ANGLE OF ATTACK AND DECREASING DRAG. WING SPEEDS UP.

(1) CONTROL STICK MOVED TO THE RIGHT

(3) NOSE SWINGS TO LEFT & GLIDER BEGINS TO ROLL LEFT

(2) LEFT AILERON MOVES DOWN INCREASING ANGLE OF ATTACK AND INCREASING DRAG. WING SLOWS DOWN.

Very Important!

Anytime you deflect the aileron downward you create aileron drag on that wing. Therefore, anytime you move the ailerons you must move the rudder!

The designers of the glider have tried to make the control movements proportional. If you move the control stick sideways one inch you will need to move the rudder pedal one inch. Move the stick halfway, and you will need one half rudder travel etc.

SUMMARY

This covers the primary flight controls. It's a lot of information you must understand thoroughly if you are to perform properly. To simplify things, consider the following. . .

There are only three primary flight controls: Elevator, Rudder, Ailerons.

As a pilot, you therefore have to do only three things:

1. Control where you are going (direction).
2. Control how fast you are going (speed).
3. Make the glider fly efficiently (coordinated).

— You control direction by controlling bank angle with the ailerons.

— You control airspeed by controlling the angle of attack of the wing with the elevator.

✳ You fly efficiently by flying the glider in a coordinated, streamlined manner with the rudder.

Here's how we do these three things...

First, control turning, the rate of turn, and thus the direction by changing the bank angle in relation to the earth's horizon. We watch the horizon to give us visual clues to see if the glider is flying straight and level, or is banked the amount we desire to make a turn.

Second, fly a steady, desired airspeed by holding the glider's nose below the horizon at a constant level, or constant pitch attitude. If the control stick is moved forward, the nose will lower to a new attitude relative to the horizon, and the glider will fly faster.

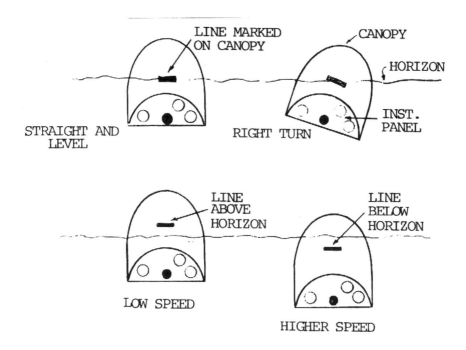

23

A skier sliding down a mountain reacts in a similar way. A shallow slope will allow the skier to coast at a slow speed and a steeper slope will cause a faster speed. Also note the skier takes time to slow down and coast to a stop at the bottom of the hill. A glider also takes time to change speeds after you establish a new pitch attitude.

Third, keep the glider streamlined with the airflow by watching a short piece of yarn fastened to the canopy. This is called a *yaw string*. The yaw string was the first aircraft instrument. It was invented by Wilbur Wright.

If the yaw string is off-center, the glider is flying sideways through the air. This creates undesirable drag when the airflow pushes against the side of the fuselage, and the air flows across the wing at an angle instead of straight across as it should. The result: an unnecessary loss of performance, the exact opposite of what we need to soar successfully. It is important to keep the yaw string straight by using the controls properly.

To remember which rudder to push to streamline the glider, think of the yaw string as an arrow. The front of the string (the part fastened) becomes the point and the free end becomes the feathers.

VIEW LOOKING FORWARD THROUGH WINDSHIELD

In the example, the yaw string is 'pointing' to the right rudder pedal. Pressing the right pedal will cause the glider fuselage to align itself with the airflow and become streamlined.

Using the Earth's horizon as a reference is the principle method to control airspeed and direction. While watching the horizon, the yaw string is easily observed. For best flying habits, avoid looking at the glider's instruments.

DECISIONS

At the end of each section of this book, you will find a decision note. When flying, you will have many decisions and judgments to make. This process begins now.

Your first decision is to make the effort to memorize all of the information about the flight controls you have just read. It is unlikely you will remember all of the information after reading it just one time.

Without the knowledge in your head, it is impossible for your hands to be able to perform properly. You will be a better, safer pilot with thorough knowledge.

FLYING LESSON NUMBER 1

The preceding concepts become easier to understand after you have experienced them, so let's go fly and see how it works...

The first lesson will consist of your instructor flying the glider on aerotow to 3,000 feet. After release, the instructor will demonstrate the use of each of the controls, and allow you to practice. After the instructor lands the glider, you will review the flight together.

During the aerotow, you may note how the control surfaces of the tow plane move very little. Hold the glider's control stick lightly and rest your feet on the rudder pedals. Note how little the instructor needs to move the controls of the glider.

As the tow plane makes a gentle turn, you can imagine 'lift arrows' coming out the top of the wing, lifting the tow plane around the turn.

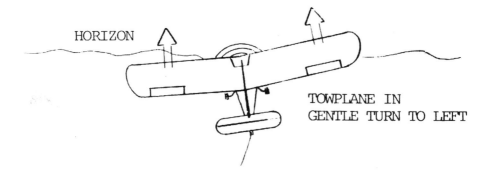

HORIZON

TOWPLANE IN GENTLE TURN TO LEFT

When the glider reaches the tow height, the instructor will probably ask you to pull the release knob with your left hand.

The instructor will turn right after release to clear the tow rope. (The glider always turns right after release, and the tow plane always turns left to avoid a collision.) The instructor then may ask you to adjust the glider's trim lever.

THE TRIM

The glider will naturally want to fly with the nose below the horizon. The amount the nose is below the horizon will depend upon the weight of the pilots on board. The trim helps to adjust for the loading of the glider and neutralizes the fore and aft stick pressures so the glider holds a steady pitch attitude and airspeed without the need to hold against the stick pressures all the time. The trim may be adjusted at any time during flight to reduce the fore and aft stick pressure.

Once the trim is set, the instructor may fly with hands off the controls to demonstrate the glider is stable. Notice how the glider flies quite well without any help! After a time, a gust of air might cause a wing to tilt and start the glider into a turn. This is an important lesson because it reminds you that as a pilot, you do only three things: control airspeed, control direction, and keep the glider fuselage streamlined. You don't 'fly' the glider. It is a common mistake for new pilots to move the controls too much.

As the wing begins to tilt or bank, the instructor will ask you to take hold of the control stick with your right hand. Hold the stick lightly. Watch the horizon.

Bring the wing level with the horizon by moving the stick opposite the tilt. You are now controlling the bank angle, and therefore you are now controlling where you are going.

If the wings are not level, you will notice the nose of the glider moving across the horizon as the glider gently turns.

Notice how the nose of the glider is below the horizon. If you hold this pitch attitude, (with the elevator) you will fly a steady speed. That's all you need to do for now. The instructor will operate the rudder while you make a gentle turn first one way then another. Make very gentle turns. Don't be aggressive.

When making a turn, you only apply the ailerons until the glider assumes the bank angle you want. As soon as the desired bank angle is attained, move the control stick back towards the middle position. If you continue to hold aileron pressure in the direction of the turn, the glider will continue to bank to steeper angles.

The amount you move the control stick sideways controls the rate the glider rolls. If you move the stick just a little to the left, the glider will slowly roll left, and will continue to slowly roll as long as you are applying stick pressure. A large movement of the stick will result in a rapid roll rate which will continue until the pilot removes the stick pressure.

When establishing a desired bank angle, first apply the amount of aileron pressure (sideways stick pressure) you desire, to effect the roll rate you want, then, as the bank angle is attained, remove the sideways stick pressure and give a small opposite pressure to stop the bank angle from increasing further.

Next, you might try changing airspeed by moving the control stick forward to a new pitch attitude to gain speed. The relationship of the nose of the glider with the horizon is called *pitch attitude*. Notice the new sound and the pressure needed on the stick to maintain this attitude. Bring the nose back up to the previous attitude, and you will fly at the same speed as before. It is important to keep the nose below the horizon at all times.

The elevator is very sensitive, so be careful not to move the control too aggressively.

You are now controlling two of the three things a pilot does. You are able to control where you are going, and how fast you are going there. Notice how a pilot uses the horizon as the primary reference to control both airspeed and direction.

AILERON DRAG

After a brief practice period, the instructor will take the controls and you will remain lightly on the controls to feel the instructor's movements. Up to now, the instructor has kept the glider streamlined (coordinated) with rudder movements to counteract the aileron drag as you moved the ailerons. Now the instructor will demonstrate the effect of aileron drag. You should direct your attention to the horizon during this demonstration.

The instructor will intentionally move the ailerons and NOT the rudder. When the stick is moved to the left, you would expect the glider to bank left and then make a left turn. This time when the ailerons are moved and not the rudder, the glider first yaws to the RIGHT! On a second demonstration, notice as the glider yaws to the right, it still banks to the left, and after a brief delay, (nearly three seconds) begins a turn to the left even without using the rudder.

The ailerons are causing two effects. One effect is the undesired yawing motion in the opposite direction from the intended turn. The other is the desired effect of causing the glider to bank, which redirects the lift and causes a turn.

During the aileron drag demonstration, notice how the yaw string goes way off center, indicating that rudder should be applied. The yaw string being off center indicates a very poor turn, one that generates lots of drag. The glider is not being flown coordinated.

Your instructor will make one last demonstration. This time, the ailerons and rudder will be applied at the same time in the proper manner. Notice how the turn is entered smoothly, the controls cause the glider to react instantly, and the yaw string stays centered, indicating a proper coordinated turn entry has been made.

Without proper use of the rudder, the glider reacts very slowly, and the fuselage is unnecessarily exposed sidewards to the relative airflow, creating a large amount of drag.

You will now be permitted to demonstrate aileron drag to yourself by banking the glider without using any rudder. (Watch the yaw string go off center, and the nose swing incorrectly through the horizon.) After this, you will practice making a few coordinated turn entries with proper use of the ailerons and rudder together. It's not easy at first.

It is very important to move just enough rudder to keep the yaw string straight anytime you move the ailerons. In most aircraft, you will probably not use *enough* rudder pressure, and the yaw string will indicate you should apply more rudder as you apply sideways stick pressure, or aileron.

Anytime you move the stick sideways, you must move the corresponding rudder pedal too. Develop the habit of responding to aileron movements with rudder movements. Do not wait until the yaw string goes crooked before responding with rudder. This is incorrect technique. The object is to keep the yaw string straight at all times.

When flying, try to rest your feet lightly on the rudder pedals. Because of the stress of the learning situation, it is a common error for new pilots to push on both rudder pedals all of the time. This makes proper rudder movements more difficult. During normal situations, a new pilot will not use enough rudder pedal movement when required.

You will find it very much easier to fly correctly when you use gentle control inputs. Gross, abrupt control motions are very difficult.

Soon you will enter the airport traffic pattern. The instructor will take over and land the glider.

During the debriefing, the instructor will review the important points of this lesson, and will fill out your log book. You will be instructed to re-read this chapter and study the next one on stability.

This first lesson may be the most important one you'll have. Your complete under-standing of this lesson is essential.

Before taking your first flying lesson, take test number 1.

WRITTEN TEST #1

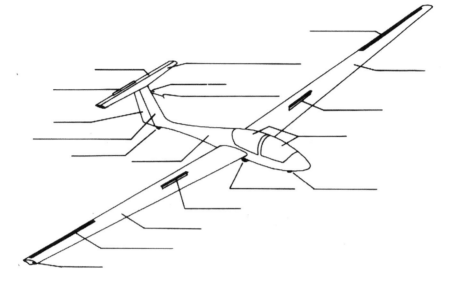

1. Nomenclature. Name all the above parts of the aircraft.

2. Why does an aircraft have . . .

a. Ailerons?

b. Elevator?

c. Rudder?

3. What does the wing do?

4. What is angle of attack?

5. Name three things that happen when angle of attack is changed.

a.

b.

c.

6. Pushing on the left rudder pedal will cause the nose of the glider to yaw which way?

7. Why does a glider have a yaw string?

8. In the following drawing, which rudder should be pressed to straighten the yaw string?

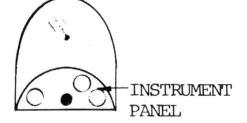

9. Before making a turn, a pilot should always

10. What turns an aircraft?

Answers on page 148

DECISIONS

You should be able to answer the questions with exact wording. Answers that are nearly correct are also nearly incorrect!

STABILITY

Designers of aircraft strive to make them easy to fly. One way they achieve this is to make the glider want to fly itself with little assistance from the pilot. This is called *stability*.

An aircraft is able to rotate about one of three axes when each of the controls is used. When you move the rudder, the glider rotates about the *yaw* or *vertical axis*. The glider *yaws*.

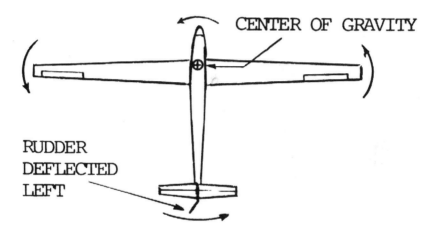

CENTER OF GRAVITY

RUDDER DEFLECTED LEFT

When the left rudder is pressed, the tail goes right and the nose goes left. The glider rotates about a point called the *center of gravity* or simply C.G., through which the three axes pass. Center of gravity is a point where, if the glider were supported it would balance and tend to remain in one position.

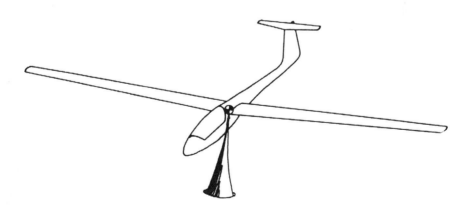

The ailerons cause the glider to roll about the *roll* or *longitudinal axis*.

UP AILERON

DOWN AILERON

The glider rolls about the C.G.

The elevator causes the glider to rotate about the *pitch* or *lateral axis*.

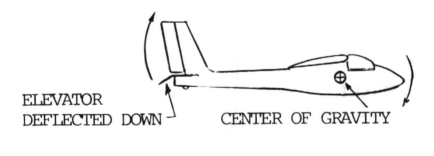

ELEVATOR
DEFLECTED DOWN

CENTER OF GRAVITY

SIDE VIEW

The three axes are generally spoken of as the roll (longitudinal), pitch (lateral), and yaw (vertical) axis.

YAW STABILITY

To understand yaw stability, think of the glider as a weather vane. Notice how little of the fuselage is in front of the C.G. and how much of the fuselage, plus the vertical stabilizer area are behind the C.G. Weathervanes are built the same way.

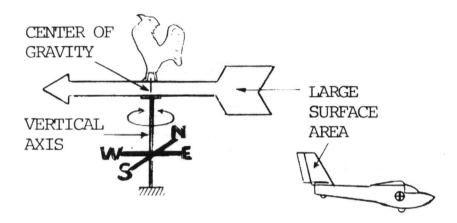

Anytime the airflow blows against the side of the glider, the glider, like a weathervane, will align itself parallel to the relative airflow, thus achieving yaw stability.

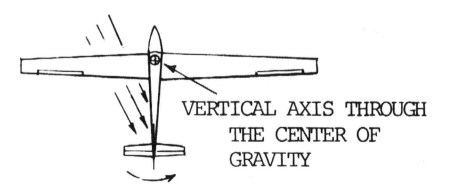

ROLL STABILITY

    Roll stability means the glider will tend to fly with its wings level with the earth. This is achieved by mounting the wings on the fuselage at an angle called *dihedral*. If you are familiar with model free-flight airplanes that have no controls or radios, you might have noticed they often have a double dihedral for extra stability.

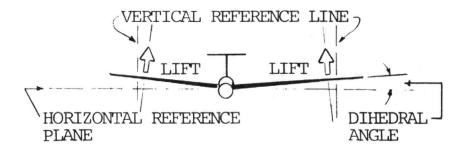

    If the glider should roll or bank, the lift is tilted too. The resulting forces cause the glider to side slip towards the lowered wing. This causes the relative airflow to strike the lowered wing more directly than the upper wing, lifting it. This causes the glider to settle back to the original level position.

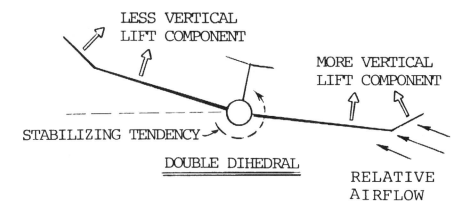

PITCH STABILITY

Pitch stability is the tendency for the glider to maintain a constant angle of attack. Pitch stability is the most difficult to explain. Let's first take another look at the airfoil. Lift is produced over nearly all of the surface of the wing. Small amounts of lift are produced at the very front (leading edge) of the airfoil, and at the trailing edge. The bulk of the lift is produced near the maximum thickness of the airfoil. The arrows in the drawing represent the amount of lift being produced over the airfoil. Joining the arrows produces a *lift distribution curve*.

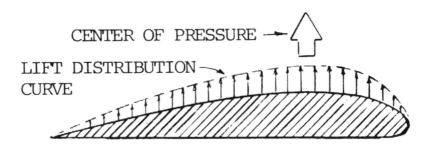

Designers of gliders average this lift and compute the point at which all lift can be considered to act, or *center of pressure* of the wing. For easier understanding, let us call this *center of lift*. Notice on the side view, the center of lift is BEHIND the center of gravity.

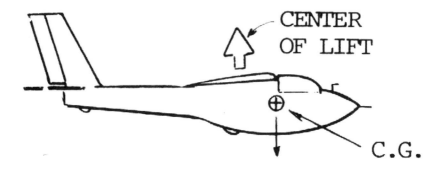

If it weren't for something else, the lift would cause the glider to rotate about the center of gravity and pitch the nose down all the time. To overcome this rotational force, the designers mount the horizontal stabilizer on the tail at a slight negative angle of attack so it produces a slight <u>downward</u> force. This downward force is just enough to overcome the rotational force caused by the center of lift being behind the C.G. The balancing act between the C.G., lift and downward force is what makes the glider stable in pitch, and therefore will want to maintain a constant angle of attack and airspeed. (Incidentally, the angle the wings and horizontal stabilizer are mounted on the fuselage is called *angle of incidence*.)

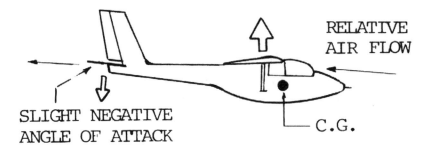

RELATIVE AIR FLOW

SLIGHT NEGATIVE ANGLE OF ATTACK

C.G.

If you should force the glider to fly at a faster speed by holding the control stick forward, the tail would produce more and more upward force. If you would then release the stick pressure, the tail would pull down, bringing the nose up. After a few oscillations, the glider would stabilize at the trimmed speed. Your instructor will allow you to experience this effect.

STUDENT FEARS

Nearly every student is afraid they will do something wrong or will allow something to happen to force the aircraft to roll upside down and fall out of the sky. This is a frightening thought, of course, but not very likely. Here's why. As the bank angle is increased, the lift is tilted. Imagine a glider tilted completely over on its side. (Drawing on next page.) Notice all of the lift is now lifting sideways! There is nothing holding the glider up, so the glider will begin to fall sideways. Actually, this flight attitude is impossible except for brief periods; the glider will begin to 'fall' long before reaching this extreme angle of bank.

As the glider begins to fall, the relative airflow begins to strike the side of the glider. (Glider 'A')

The yaw stability now begins to take effect. The tail will be caused to yaw up and the nose will yaw down. (Glider 'B') When the nose yaws down, the lift will now be directed ahead of the glider and will lift the nose back up to level flight due to pitch stability. (Glider 'C')

The glider will tend to return to a normal gliding attitude and airspeed after a short oscillation even if pilot control is not applied.

Remember, because of the stability that is designed into every aircraft, the glider is built to fly, and in many cases does a better, smoother job than some pilots! We don't 'fly' aircraft. All we do is control where we are going, (direction), how fast we go, (airspeed), and keep the glider flying streamlined (coordinated).

(Glider in 90 degree bank.)

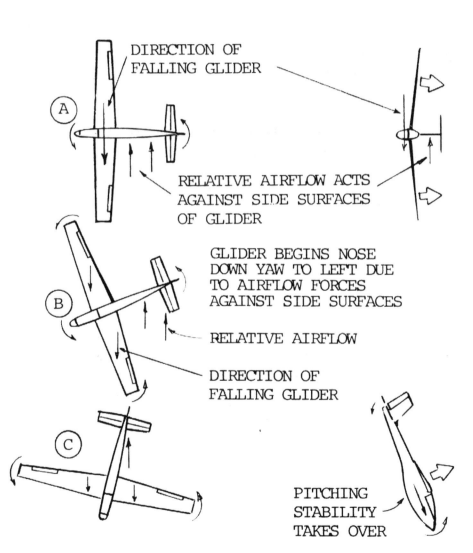

A — DIRECTION OF FALLING GLIDER

RELATIVE AIRFLOW ACTS AGAINST SIDE SURFACES OF GLIDER

B — GLIDER BEGINS NOSE DOWN YAW TO LEFT DUE TO AIRFLOW FORCES AGAINST SIDE SURFACES

RELATIVE AIRFLOW

DIRECTION OF FALLING GLIDER

C — PITCHING STABILITY TAKES OVER

GLIDER IN 90 DEGREE BANK

WRITTEN TEST #2 - STABILITY

1. Name the three axes of the glider.

a.

b.

c.

2. When the glider moves about any axis, it rotates about the _____ __ _____.

3. The glider fuselage tends to fly streamlined through the relative airflow because of the _____ effect and thus is stable about the yaw (vertical) axis.

4. The glider tends to fly with its wings level because the wings are mounted on the fuselage at an angle called _____.

5. Pitch stability is achieved by a balancing act between the horizontal stabilizer, wing lift, and the _____ __ _____.

Answers on page 149

DECISIONS

In all of your flying lessons, perhaps none are as important as the first two. The information you have learned will affect all of your future flying. Your complete understanding of all the information is paramount to your future satisfaction and safety. If you have any doubts or questions, ask your instructor for further explanations or practice. You play an important part in the learning process.

FLIGHT NUMBER TWO

This will be another 3,000 foot tow. You'll practice speed control and coordination of the rudder with the ailerons in turns. Notice again how little control movement is necessary.

Beginning with this lesson you must look for any other aircraft in the direction you are going to turn BEFORE you begin the turn. This is commonly called "clearing the turn".

Clearing is the first step of ALL turns to prevent collisions with other aircraft.

On the next pages you will find a pre-takeoff checklist you must memorize. You will be shown how to use the checklist after you are in the cockpit and have the seat belts fastened.

The instructor may allow you to try part of the aerotow if conditions are very calm. Remember to adjust the trim. You don't have to adjust the trim, but it will help you fly a steady airspeed.

The principle purpose of this lesson is to allow you to practice turn entries and recoveries.

After clearing the turn, try to enter the turn with appropriate aileron and rudder movements. It is much easier to perform gentle turn entries rather than using brisk, aggressive control movements. As you apply control inputs, the glider will react instantly. If the yaw string indicates you used too much, or too little rudder to counteract aileron drag properly, adjust the rudder movement to make the yaw string become straight as soon as you can.

Remember to clear the area before recovering from a turn. Recovery from turns requires the same aileron and rudder coordination as turn entries in order to keep the yaw string straight.

You will practice numerous turn entries and recoveries so you can develop proper rudder usage and keep the yaw string straight. Your instructor must be satisfied you understand the proper control inputs to enter and recover from a turn before advancing on to the next training phase. Along with the yaw string, you will notice how the nose of the glider swings across the horizon when the rudder is used properly.

To maintain a constant airspeed, remember to watch the horizon and NOT the airspeed indicator! If you keep the nose of the glider at a constant pitch attitude by keeping the nose below the horizon at a constant spacing, the airspeed will stay constant.

One of the interesting things an instructor might do to improve a student's airspeed control, is to cover the airspeed indicator entirely! This forces the student to watch the horizon, and the airspeed stays constant!

Watching outside the glider is very important. The pilot then is able to simultaneously watch for other aircraft, control the bank angle and airspeed better, watch the yaw string, and see where the likely best thermals or other thermalling gliders are.

You will practice many turn entries and recoveries. You may also perform turns that may continue through 90° or more of arc.

USING THE RUDDER DURING TURNS

During a sustained turn, if the angle of bank is not proper, you need to apply appropriate aileron pressure along with the rudder to coordinate the controls.

However, if the angle of bank is correct, and the yaw string shows the glider is not flying streamlined, it is proper to make an adjustment with the rudder alone.

The rule then is to always use the rudder anytime the ailerons are used. But, there are times when the rudder is used alone to make corrections.

The steps of a turn

1. Clear before turning by looking primarily in the direction of the turn.

2. Check the nose-below-the-horizon attitude.

3. While watching the horizon, apply stick and rudder together in the desired direction.

4. Watch the yaw string and horizon for an indication you applied the proper rudder pressure. Make an adjustment of the rudder pressure if necessary.

5. Check the nose-below-the-horizon attitude and apply back stick pressure to maintain pitch attitude.

6. As the desired bank angle is reached, reduce aileron and rudder pressures.

While in the turn.

1. Continue to watch for other nearby aircraft, while maintaining proper pitch attitude.

2. Watch the yaw string for indications the glider is flying in a coordinated manner. Adjust the yaw string with rudder pressure only, as long as the bank angle is correct.

3. Adjust aileron pressure to maintain desired bank angle. If ailerons are moved, be sure to also move rudder.

To recover from the turn.

1. Clear in the direction the glider will straighten to.

2. Remove bank angle by applying both aileron and rudder pressure.

3. Watch the yaw string and horizon to determine if proper rudder pressure is being used.

4. Watch horizon to maintain nose-below-the-horizon attitude with the elevator.

5. Centralize controls as the wings come to a level attitude.

6. Re-check nose attitude and airspeed.

As soon as you are able to hold a reasonably steady airspeed and make coordinated shallow turns, you will proceed to the next phase. Each student will progress at their own pace from this flight on.

Tip: While in a turn, many pilots find it easier to turn their head slightly so they look a little to the side. Try looking about 30 degrees in the direction of the turn. This allows you to see the wing tip with peripheral vision as the turn progresses, as well as the nose of the glider relative to the horizon, and the yaw string.

CLEARING TURNS

Pilots must always be watchful for other aircraft. An effective scan is performed by systematically focusing on different segments of the sky for short intervals (1 or 2 seconds per segment).

First look in the direction of the turn, raising or lowering the glider's wing to view above and below.

Look in the direction opposite the turn as far as possible, then scan from segment to segment, looking up and down in each segment until you return to the direction you are turning.

Breaking the sky into segments is better than allowing your eyes to sweep across the sky in a continuous scan. You can try this as you sit in a room. Try scanning by moving your head continuously, and you will see that objects are not focused while your head is moving. Also, your eyes will automatically jerk from point to point as you try to make a continuous scan, missing important areas.

Before making any turn, or unusual maneuvers such as stalls, the pilot is required to look in all directions for any conflicting aircraft.

PRE-TAKEOFF CHECKLIST

Before each takeoff, the pilot must be sure the glider is ready for flight. To do this in a systematic order, we use a checklist printed by the manufacturer placed in the cockpit of all modern sailplanes. Some gliders have very peculiar items that must be checked before each flight, and the manufacturer is sure to put these items in the written checklist. On the other hand, many gliders were constructed before it was required to have a manufacturers written checklist. All glider pilots must, therefore, have a memorized checklist to use in these conditions.

The following checklist is the most widely used checklist in the English speaking world. It easily remembered with the letters CB SIT CBE.

C Controls - Check all controls for freedom of movement and proper takeoff position.

B Ballast - Check for proper weight and balance and any required ballast is secure.

S Straps - Seat belts secure and snug.

I Instruments - Adjusted and proper reading.

T Trim - Set for takeoff.

C Canopy - Closed and locked.

B Brakes - Closed and locked.

E Emergency plan.

Unfortunately, some manufacturer's written checklists do not include all of the important memorized items. Because of this, first perform the written checklist, and then mentally go through the CB-SIT-CBE checklist to be sure all items are covered.

A manufacturer's written checklist may include important items not included in the memorized one, so the written checklist takes precedence. Since the written checklist may not include all of the important items of the memorized checklist, it too must be performed. Many pilots print a pre-takeoff checklist including items from both the manufacturer and the standard memorized list.

The normal manner is to perform the written cockpit checklist, then review the memorized one to ensure all items were covered. There is usually no need to re-do the items.

When several flights are made, such as pattern tows, the pilot must go through the entire checklist on each flight in proper sequence so nothing is overlooked.

DECISIONS

The majority of soaring accidents fall into only a few categories. Some of the most common problems are the result of incomplete, or inadequate pre-takeoff checklists. Never allow a takeoff to occur until the entire checklist has been accomplished. Never allow others to distract you while you are performing the checklist.

SHALLOW, MEDIUM
AND STEEP TURNS

Until now, you have performed only shallow turns. You will now learn how the controls are used in various turns and then practice some steeper turns.

It is common for students to be told in order to perform a turn, you apply aileron and rudder until the bank angle is established, and then return the controls to the "neutral" position. The student soon discovers when a turn is established, if the controls are brought back to a true neutral position, the glider will want to become more or less banked, and the yaw string will tend to go off center. The student applies whatever control is necessary to stabilize the glider, then neutralizes the controls again only to find the glider wandering again. This constant adjustment is less efficient than if the pilot holds the controls in a correct position during turns.

Here is an explanation of what the glider wants to do, why it happens, and how the controls must be held during a turn:

In the stability chapter you learned a glider wants to fly level because of roll stability. If you roll the glider into a gentle bank angle and then neutralize the controls, the glider is designed to want to roll to a level position. Therefore, in a shallow turn you will need to hold a very slight amount of aileron pressure into the turn to overcome the roll stability. The amount of pressure in this case is hardly noticeable.

In a steep turn another factor comes into play. It's called the *overbanking tendency*. During a steep turn, the outboard wing is travelling a greater distance than the inboard wing and therefore must travel at a faster speed.

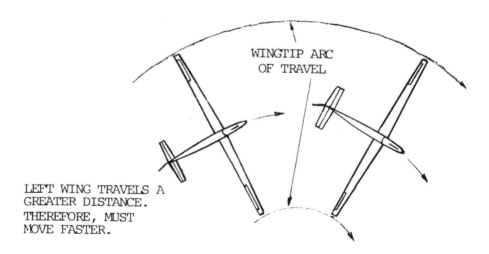

WINGTIP ARC
OF TRAVEL

LEFT WING TRAVELS A
GREATER DISTANCE.
THEREFORE, MUST
MOVE FASTER.

The increased airflow over the outboard wing causes it to produce more lift than the inboard wing. The glider wants to become more steeply banked. In a steep turn, you will need to hold aileron pressure *against* the turn to overcome the overbanking tendency. This effect is very noticeable.

45

Of course, there is a medium turn where stability and the overbanking tendency just balance out and the control stick will be in the middle.

In all turns, some rudder must be used in the direction of the turn.

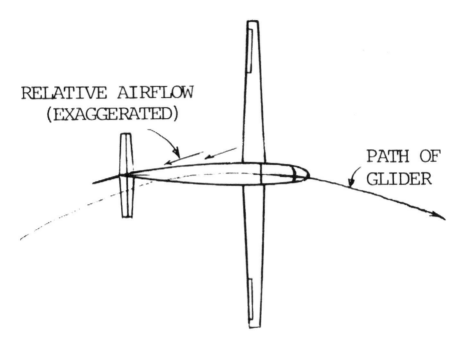

RELATIVE AIRFLOW
(EXAGGERATED)

PATH OF
GLIDER

Imagine a glider with a fuselage 1,000 feet long. There is only one point on the aircraft that is exactly on the arc of the turn. That point is the Center of Gravity of the glider. All other points on the aircraft are either to the left or the right of the arc of the turn.

In normal, coordinated flight, the tail of the glider is outside the arc of the turn. The relative airflow tries to push the tail towards the inside of the turn. In order to keep the yaw string straight, and the air flowing over the wings in the most efficient manner, the pilot must use a slight, but discernible amount of rudder pressure in the direction of the turn.

In gentle, shallow turns the need for rudder pressure is hardly noticeable. In steeper turns, you will find a definite amount of rudder pressure is required.

The following drawing helps to understand proper rudder usage.

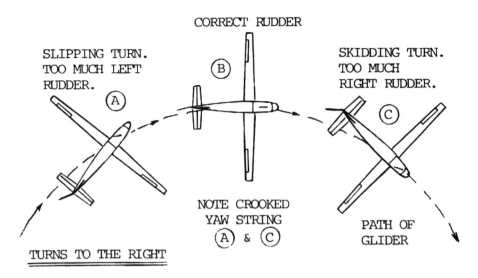

CORRECT RUDDER

SLIPPING TURN.
TOO MUCH LEFT
RUDDER.

SKIDDING TURN.
TOO MUCH
RIGHT RUDDER.

NOTE CROOKED
YAW STRING
(A) & (C)

PATH OF
GLIDER

TURNS TO THE RIGHT

To summarize:

All turns begin with aileron and rudder applied in the direction of the turn. Once the desired angle of bank is established, you will return the controls towards the neutral position, but in order to hold a steady turn, you will need to hold:

In a shallow turn — aileron INTO the turn, rudder into the turn.

In a medium turn — aileron neutral, rudder into the turn.

In a steep turn — aileron AGAINST the turn, rudder into the turn.

THE ELEVATOR IN THE TURN

Another thing you will notice: As you bank the glider into a turn, the nose of the glider wants to go down, and the glider wants to speed up. As we have seen, because of built-in stability, a glider has a tendency to keep itself at a constant angle of attack.

During any turn, a glider weighs more than straight and level flight because of centrifugal force. (Centrifugal force is what keeps water in a bucket when you swing it over your head.) The glider's wings need to produce additional lift in order to sustain this added weight.

If the glider is to fly at the same speed during a turn as it did in straight flight, it would need a higher angle of attack to produce more lift. Since the glider's built in stability keeps the angle of attack constant, (not airspeed) the glider will want to increase speed (more airflow over the wing) to produce the required lift to offset the increased weight during a turn.

In order to keep the airspeed constant during turns, the glider pilot needs to increase the angle of attack with the elevator by increased back pressure on the stick — often a *lot* of back pressure. In a very steep turn, the control stick may be held fully back against the stop. This will be demonstrated later during your flight training.

When entering a turn, stability causes the nose of the glider to go down a few seconds after the turn is begun. (It takes a moment for centrifugal force to cause increased weight.) Increased back stick pressure is only required a few seconds after the turn is begun. Perform a turn entry without applying any back stick pressure and watch the horizon for the nose of the glider to begin to lower by itself. This will typically occur after the glider has turned as much as 30 degrees into the turn.

If you anticipate the need for back stick pressure by applying the control too early, the nose will raise above the correct position, causing the glider to slow below the desired airspeed, followed by the nose dropping well below the correct position with the airspeed then too fast. (A common pilot error.)

To maintain a constant, correct airspeed as you enter a turn, watch the horizon and keep the pitch attitude constant as the bank angle is increased. Be aware that some back stick pressure will be needed, but wait until the proper moment to apply it.

DECISIONS

The mark of a good pilot is one who can make a coordinated turn at a constant speed. It takes lots of practice, but this skill should be your goal.

WRITTEN TEST #3

SHALLOW, MEDIUM AND STEEP TURNS

1. When a pilot 'flies' an aircraft, only three things are being controlled. They are:

a.

b.

c.

2. In a shallow turn, the pilot will need to hold some aileron (into, against) _____ the turn because of the _____ stability.

3. In a steep turn, the pilot will need to hold some aileron (into, against) _____ the turn because of the _____ tendency.

4. During all turns, some _____ will be needed in the direction of the turn.

Answers on page 149

GROUND HANDLING

Sailplanes are built to be light in weight but strong too. The designers must take into consideration the loads put on the sailplane during ground handling.

Especially weak areas include: All control surfaces, the trailing edge of the wing, and all of the fabric and skin of the aircraft. The nose of the fuselage of many sailplanes is thin metal or fiberglass, so no pressure should be put on this area. In many cases, wing tip wheels should not be used to pull the glider, nor to tie it down.

Places usually strong enough for handling include: Special handling bars or handles, some wing tips, the leading edge of the wing, and wing struts. The glider should not be moved forward or backwards using the wing tips if the ground is soft, or great effort is required. Pulling the glider by the wing tips can cause damage to the wing root area, or the connections in the fuselage.

Use special care when pushing some gliders backwards. If the elevator is very close to the ground, it can be damaged. Be sure to lift the tail, tie the stick back or pull the trim full back to hold the elevator up when pushing these gliders backwards.

Never leave a canopy open and unattended. If the canopy falls, or the wind blows it shut, it may crack. While preflighting the exterior of the glider be sure to close and lock the canopy.

On gliders with a sliding glass window in the canopy, do not lift up or push down on the window opening. The plastic slide rails are very fragile and expensive, plus you can easily break the canopy. Open a canopy by lifting on the frame or other strong structure.

You will be shown how to properly tie down the sailplane and lock the controls for protection from wind damage.

Never leave the sailplane unattended if it is not tied down. Unexpected gusts on otherwise calm days have destroyed sailplanes while helpless onlookers watched in horror!

The minimum effort on reasonably calm days is to place an old tire or other weight on the upwind wing tip, while the glider is positioned with it's nose pointed across the wind.

The last pilot in command of the glider is always responsible for it's security.

When towing a glider with a vehicle, the tow rope should be more than 1/2 wingspan, and there should be at least a person at each wing tip. If there are windy conditions, or the glider is being towed downhill, more people should be placed on the nose and tail of the glider. In severe conditions, a pilot may also have to be placed in the glider to help control it while being towed. In strong conditions, it may be wise to leave the glider tied down rather than attempting to move it. Always be sure to have an adequate number of people.

PREFLIGHT

Inspecting the glider before flight is commonly called a *preflight inspection*. The Federal Aviation Agency (FAA) considers all preparations for flight to be included in a preflight inspection, including checking weather conditions, reviewing maps for a cross country flight, and other matters not involving the actual checking of the aircraft. The FAA considers the inspection of the aircraft to be a "Line Inspection". For the purpose of this manual, we will use the generic term, preflight, to mean the inspection of the glider only. However, you should understand there are other preflight considerations for safe flight preparation.

The aircraft flight manual will specify those items that must be checked on a preflight inspection. Your instructor will show you how to preflight the particular sailplane you are going to use in your training program. The following generalizations apply to all sailplanes.

You are inspecting the sailplane for three reasons:

1. Is it assembled properly?

2. Is it in good condition and has no hidden damage?

3. Is it legal to fly?

The Federal Government, through the FAA, has given glider pilots special permission to disassemble their sailplanes. A power pilot is not allowed to remove a wing (only a licensed aircraft mechanic is permitted to do this). The FAA recognizes the special nature of soaring and allows us to do what the power pilot may not.

This privilege carries with it the responsibility to be very sure not only that the pilot is competent to perform an assembly and disassembly, but also to recognize when the sailplane has not been assembled properly by someone else.

Read the aircraft flight manual carefully. It will explain how to assemble the sailplane and what important items to inspect during the preflight.

An aircraft must have certain documents to meet federal regulations. You can remember these required documents by knowing that all aircraft must have an OAR on board.

O - Operating limitations in the form of the owners manual or placards including weight and balance data.

A - Airworthiness Certificate.

R - Registration Certificate.

The airworthiness certificate is issued to the aircraft when it was new. The certificate states that this type of aircraft is licensed in a particular category (normal, utility, aerobatic). It is not a certificate to show this particular aircraft is airworthy. The airworthiness certificate never expires.

The registration certificate shows who owns the aircraft, and is only changed when ownership changes.

HIDDEN DAMAGE

A damaged aircraft may be unsafe to fly. Such damage can be caused by landing hard, handling the glider improperly, exceeding the structural limits by flying too fast, using the controls improperly, or something bumping into it on the ground.

Pay particular attention to wrinkled or cracked skin near the landing gear and the tail forward of the vertical stabilizer (hard landing or ground loop) or on the wing and tail surfaces (excessive in-flight maneuvering). Excessive use of the controls at high speeds might show up as bent or cracked hinge attach points on the ailerons, rudder or elevator. Damaged dive brake hinges or a slightly bent dive brake might indicate use at excessive speeds.

Loose rivets (popped rivets) or wrinkled metal between the rivets, caused by over-stressing a part of the glider, would indicate possible internal damage. Pay close attention to the space between the rivets for evidence of buckling of the metal which may indicate overstressing.

Damage also can occur when the sailplane is bumped into something or when someone falls against the aircraft.

CRITTERS

The inside of an aircraft makes a great home for porcupines, skunks, and other furry animals as well as snakes, hornets and wasps! The pitot tube seems to be a great home for spiders and wasps. Mice chew on seat belts for the salt left by human perspiration, and they also chew electrical wiring insulation.

MISCELLANEOUS

The airspeed indicator and variometer instruments should read '0', the glass face unbroken, and the altimeter should be able to be adjusted to the field elevation with a proper barometric setting in the 'window' of the altimeter.

The release hook should be clean and in good condition. The backward release spring (if so equipped) should have obvious tension. Inspect the area around the release mechanism for signs of overstressing.

The spaces under and behind the seat cushions should be checked for ballast weights. Remove any that aren't needed. Secure or remove any loose objects.

You are responsible for the condition of the tow rope.

If you find any discrepancy, bring it to the attention of your flight instructor.

PREFLIGHT CHECKLIST

There are many items to be checked on a preflight inspection. It is easy to overlook or forget an item. You may be distracted while performing the preflight inspection, or you may be rushed and not perform a complete inspection. Many accidents could have been prevented by the pilot noticing some problem during a thorough preflight inspection.

Some sailplanes can have a particular item that must be checked before flight that applies to only that sailplane.

The manufacturer is required to provide a written preflight checklist. Using this checklist on every preflight is the best way to perform a complete, thorough preflight inspection. By using a written checklist, the pilot is more sure of checking all important items. Most gliders keep the written checklist on board. Use it on every preflight inspection! If the glider does not have a written checklist on board, ask for the flight manual, and use the factory preflight checklist.

THE POSITIVE CONTROL CHECK

One common accident is for a glider pilot to take off with one of the controls not connected. During the preflight inspection, you will be shown how to perform a *positive control check*. This is done by having one person hold a control surface while another puts pressure first one way then the other, on the entire control actuating mechanism by trying to move the control from inside the cockpit with the control stick or other control handle. If the control were not connected properly a looseness would be felt. Don't be so aggressive with the positive control check that you damage the glider!

WEIGHT AND BALANCE

If the glider is to fly properly, it must be within correct weight and balance limits. It must balance properly. Each aircraft has a weight and balance sheet in it's records. Most gliders also have a placard in the cockpit that will apply in most, but not all, situations. If the placard does not cover your situation, you will have to refer to the weight and balance sheet.

The placard on some gliders, such as the Schweizer 2-33, can be confusing, and easily interpreted incorrectly. Be sure an instructor reviews the weight and balance data on any glider with which you are not familiar.

THE WALK-AROUND INSPECTION

Suppose you preflight the glider, fly, land and then go to lunch. A short time later you return and find the glider hasn't been flown during your absence.

You may not need to do a complete preflight, but you should walk around the glider looking for any damage or for control locks that might have been put on to prevent wind damage during your absence. Another positive control check would be a good idea. If there is any possibility that someone may have been probing around the glider, a complete preflight inspection is in order.

DISTRACTIONS

Many glider accidents are the result of a pilot being distracted while performing vital assembly and preflight checks. Do not allow onlookers to distract you. Politely ask them to wait until you are finished. If you observe someone distracting another pilot while they are performing checks, you can play a major role in safety by suggesting they move away from the pilot.

DECISIONS

Improper preflight inspections are the cause of many glider accidents. Do not permit anyone to disrupt you while you perform this important inspection.

WRITTEN TEST #4 - PREFLIGHT

1. What is meant by 'popped' rivets?

2. What would cause a popped rivet?

3. What are some common signs of possible hidden damage?

4. What should you look for when checking the tow release mechanism?

5. What would distorted hinges on the ailerons or dive brakes indicate?

6. What should a student pilot do if evidence of damage or excessive wear is found?

7. What documents are required in a glider?

8. What should you look for when checking the pitot tube?

9. How can you insure that you check every important preflight item?

10. Who is responsible for checking the tow rope before each flight?

Answers on page 150

THIS SIGNAL MAY BE CHANGED BY THE SSA TO INDICATE THERE IS SOMETHING WRONG WITH THE GLIDER, SUCH AS THE DIVE BRAKES BEING OPEN.

STANDARD AMERICAN SOARING SIGNALS

Launching safety requires clear signals, predictable intentions, and plans for emergency action.

AEROTOW TAKEOFF

WIND

One item that is not in the standard CB-SIT-CBE memorized pre-takeoff checklist, (because it is normally considered to be a pre-flight item) is to check the windsock before the launch begins.

An aircraft should takeoff into the wind for better control, and a steeper takeoff climb angle. The wind can change during the day, and you must always be aware of the wind direction. Before taking the glider to the takeoff end of the runway, check the windsock for the direction. Also, before beginning the actual takeoff, it is a good idea to make a last minute check of the wind direction.

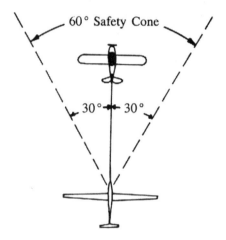

After you finish the cockpit checklist, have a qualified person connect the tow rope. Check the windsock one last time. Be sure no one is near the glider or the tow plane, and there is plenty of room to the sides in case of a ground-loop.

PROCEED WITH LAUNCH

Give the wing tip runner a thumbs-up signal with your left hand to indicate you are ready. The wing runner should look around to be sure no aircraft are on final approach, give the 'take up slack' signal and, when the tow rope is taut, look at the pilot again to receive an indication the pilot is ready to be launched, before giving the 'go' signal.

While this is happening, watch the tow rope as the slack is being taken up to see no knots form. (Any knot will reduce the strength of the rope up to 50%.) Also, watch the wing runner to be sure that person is watching for traffic. You are in a particularly awkward situation since you can't see behind the glider.

When the slack in the tow rope is all out, you should waggle the rudder of the glider as a signal to the tow pilot that you are ready to proceed with the launch, and/or give a "proceed with launch" radio call to the tow plane. At the same time, the wing runner gives the 'go' signal if the traffic pattern is clear, and all else is in readiness.

Before beginning the launch, the tow pilot is watching for both your rudder waggle, indicating you and the glider are ready, and the wing runner's go signal, indicating the traffic is clear and the rope is taut. If the launch should begin before you are ready, release immediately.

Everyone in the area of glider launching is responsible for safety. If someone detects a safety problem, they should yell "STOP" as loudly as they can. If the pilot of the glider hears someone yell "stop" they should release immediately.

Many glider operations and clubs modify this procedure because of different circumstances. Be sure to follow your instructor's procedures. Aircraft radios can make the launch procedure safer.

THE TAKEOFF ROLL

Hold the control stick lightly with the right hand. During the ground roll, the ailerons and rudder are used independently. At the beginning of the tow, keep the wings level with course movements of the ailerons, using no rudder. If there is a crosswind, keep the upwind wing slightly low. Steer the glider on the ground with the rudder using no ailerons. Once the glider becomes airborne, the controls are then used in a coordinated fashion.

As the speed increases, the controls will become more effective. As soon as possible, use the elevator to balance the glider on it's main wheel. It is important not to keep the glider on the ground longer than necessary, by holding the control stick too far forward, nor to force it off the ground too soon with excessive back stick pressure.

New pilots, or even experienced pilots flying a new type of glider, have a problem knowing just how far to bring the stick back to make the glider takeoff, and also how rapidly to move the stick, or even when to move the stick back. If the control stick is moved back too far before the wings are generating enough lift, the glider will not respond until there is enough air flowing over the wings, and then rapidly begin a climb as the lift increases, threatening to climb well above a normal tow position.

If the pilot holds the control stick too far forward during the early phase of the tow, the wings will have a great amount of airflow, and when the pilot moves the control stick back to a positive angle of attack, the glider may leap into the air and climb to an excessively high altitude.

With the glider climbing very fast, threatening to climb above the normal tow position, the glider pilot will tend to over-react by moving the control stick too far forward to prevent the glider from becoming dangerously high. It is possible for the glider to contact the ground, damaging the glider, and bouncing it back into the air.

This series of oscillations is called P.I.O.'s — Pilot Induced Oscillations, and can be very dangerous.

There is a natural impatience that makes a pilot want to get the aircraft into the air as soon as possible. However, the glider will not take off until there is enough lift generated. Lift is a function of angle of attack, and the speed of the relative airflow over the wing.

At the beginning of the tow, if the pilot holds the control stick too far aft, the glider will still not take off until the airflow is great enough. Most modern tow planes accelerate quickly, so the airflow increases rapidly. If the stick is held far back, the glider can suddenly leap into the air suddenly and continue to climb very quickly. This might cause the tail of the tow plane to be lifted, preventing the tow plane from becoming airborne, or worse, driving the tow plane into the ground. Towpilots have died in just this manner. If the glider gets too high anytime during the tow, the tow plane pilot is quite justified in releasing the tow rope.

AN EASY ANSWER

To avoid these problems, before signalling to proceed with the launch, the glider pilot should set the elevator by holding the control stick at the approximate position that will result in a proper angle of attack. To do this, move the control stick the full allowable travel fore and aft, and then find the mid-point, or neutral position. Move the control stick back about 1/2 inch from this neutral position. This will be very close to the optimum position for takeoff. Aircraft designers build aircraft this way.

Hold the stick at this position while the tow plane accelerates. Large lateral movements of the control stick may be necessary to keep the wings level, but try very hard not to move the stick fore and aft as the glider accelerates. There is a strong tendency for some people to pull back on the control stick in a futile attempt to make the glider takeoff.

Since the angle of attack is now set, the wings will generate more and more lift as the speed of the relative airflow increases. The glider will takeoff as soon as conditions are right. After takeoff, the tow plane will continue to accelerate, creating a stronger airflow, and more lift. Soon after the moment of takeoff, the control stick will probably have to be moved forward slightly (1/4 to 1/2 inch) to keep the glider from climbing too high.

After a few takeoffs, a student pilot will realize the proper stick position, and takeoffs will be easy.

After takeoff, the glider must be held just a few feet above the ground as the tow plane accelerates to its takeoff speed. Normally, the tow plane will become airborne after the glider. If the tow plane takes off before the glider, the glider pilot probably delayed the glider from taking off by holding the control stick too far forward.

The glider should be held 3 to 6 feet above the ground as the tow plane accelerates. This altitude should prevent accidental contacts with the ground, while still being safe for the tow pilot. After the tow plane becomes airborne, the towpilot will hold the tow plane level, just above the ground, allowing the airspeed to increase to the climbing speed. When the climb speed is reached, the tow plane will then be seen to begin its climb. Only then should the glider move to the normal high tow position slightly above the tow plane's propwash.

Some tow planes have enough power that this process happens very quickly. Weaker tow planes take a much longer time. The glider pilot must expect differences in tow planes and even towpilot styles that will change the towing procedure slightly.

> The glider pilot must be prepared to release the tow rope at any time if things don't appear to be going right. For this reason, the glider pilot should always have the left hand ready to pull the release knob.

CROSSWIND TAKEOFFS

The wing runner should keep the upwind wing slightly low. This will help to prevent the wind from getting under the upwind wing and forcing the glider's downwind wing onto the ground.

During the ground roll, hold slight aileron pressure into the wind, to keep the upwind wing low. This will help prevent the wind from drifting the glider sideways.

The crosswind will cause the glider to want to swerve, or weathervane into the wind. For this reason, it may be best for the wing runner to hold the downwind wing tip during the launch.

Since the crosswind will try to weathervane the glider into the wind, hold downwind rudder (downwind rudder pedal pressed forward) to help prevent the weathervaning.

Aircraft have maximum crosswind capabilities. It is common for many gliders to not be able to takeoff with more than a 15 knot direct crosswind. Beyond this crosswind strength, the rudder is not effective enough to prevent the glider from swerving into the wind, so the pilot cannot keep the glider moving straight. This maximum crosswind capability is listed in the glider's flight manual, and you should be familiar with it.

A higher than normal takeoff speed is desirable to make a clean takeoff. This will help prevent the glider from settling back to the ground.

The glider will normally become airborne before the tow plane. Once airborne, the wind will tend to drift the glider sideways, causing it to pull on the tow plane's tail sideways. This may cause the tow plane pilot to be unable to keep the tow plane going in a straight line.

The glider pilot must 'crab' the glider sideways into the wind with the rudder to offset the wind drift and maintain position directly behind the tow plane. The upwind wing can still be held slightly low, but caution must be used to prevent the wing from being so low that it threatens to contact the ground.

After the tow plane becomes airborne, both the tow plane and the glider must crab sideways along the runway to prevent being drifted downwind of the runway. It is important, however, for the glider pilot to fly directly behind the tow plane in proper position once the tow plane is airborne.

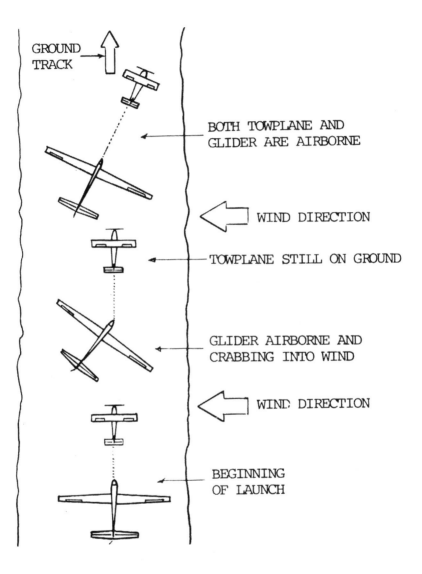

GROUND
TRACK

BOTH TOWPLANE AND
GLIDER ARE AIRBORNE

WIND DIRECTION

TOWPLANE STILL ON GROUND

GLIDER AIRBORNE AND
CRABBING INTO WIND

WIND DIRECTION

BEGINNING
OF LAUNCH

AEROTOW

As soon as you are able to make reasonably well coordinated turns and show complete understanding of the control functions during free-flight, you will attempt aerotow. Aerotow is one of the most difficult parts of the training program. You will start out by successfully controlling the glider only a few seconds before you get out of position. The instructor will take over and return the glider to the correct position so you can try again. Soon you will be able to control the glider for longer and longer periods until finally you are able to perform the entire aerotow.

Correct tow position behind the tow plane looks like this:

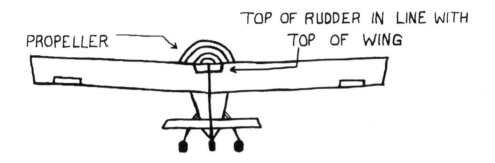

The main indication you are in the correct position is the top of the tow plane's rudder is approximately lined up with the top of its wing or canopy. This is the high tow position. The glider is slightly above the tow plane's propwash, or air turbulence caused by the rotating propeller. You may wish to test for the proper tow position by moving lower until you feel the turbulence of the propwash. Move slightly above this position and note the 'picture' you see through the windshield of the glider.

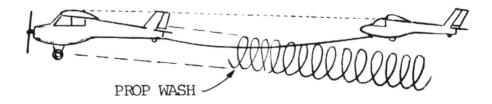

If you get too high, the top of the tow plane's rudder will appear to go down the tow plane's wing.

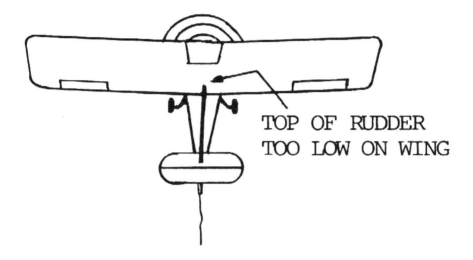

TOP OF RUDDER
TOO LOW ON WING

If you get too low, the rudder will stick up above the tow plane's wing and you may feel the turbulence of the tow plane's wake.

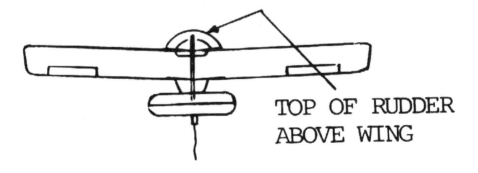

TOP OF RUDDER
ABOVE WING

There are other indicators you are flying in the proper position. The tow plane should appear in the windshield of the glider just above the instrument cowling. The exact position will differ slightly with different gliders. Also, the tow plane will appear on, or slightly above the horizon. The horizon reference may not be reliable in very hazy conditions, with powerful tow planes, or in places the horizon is not level, as in mountainous terrain.

The entire 'picture' is more important than any one of the methods used to locate the glider in the proper tow position.

Flying straight, you will be able to barely see both sides of the tow plane's fuselage. If you drift out of position to one side, you will be able to see only one side of the tow plane's fuselage.

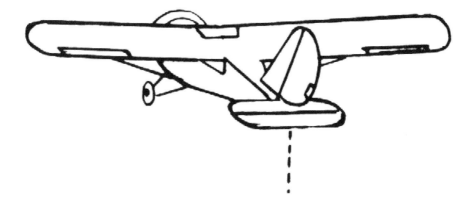

During aerotow, keep the glider's wings parallel to the wings of the tow plane. During a turn, the glider's wing should be at the same angle of bank as the tow plane's. If the glider's bank angle is steeper, the glider will want to turn quicker than the tow plane, and if the glider's bank angle is shallower than the tow plane's, the glider will not turn as quickly, and soon will be out of proper tow position.

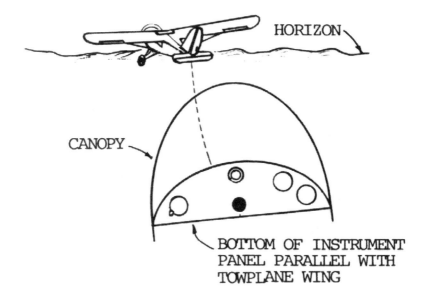

During a turn you must fly on the same arc as the tow plane. If you are in the correct position during a turn, the glider will point toward the tow plane's outside wing tip, and you will be able to see only the side of the tow plane's fuselage to the inside of the turn. You still line up the top of the tow plane's rudder with the top of its wing during a turn.

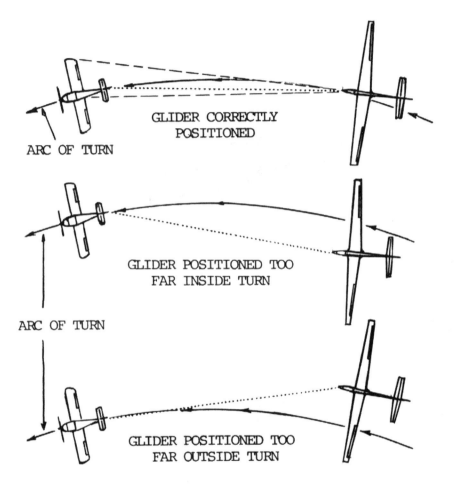

GLIDER CORRECTLY
POSITIONED

ARC OF TURN

GLIDER POSITIONED TOO
FAR INSIDE TURN

ARC OF TURN

GLIDER POSITIONED TOO
FAR OUTSIDE TURN

Remember lesson number one, the aileron drag demonstration? It took three seconds for the glider to respond when inadequate rudder was used. The glider responds instantly when the controls are used correctly — that is coordinated. On aerotow, things happen fast and you don't have three extra seconds. Use co-ordinated control movements and be particularly sure to use enough rudder to make the glider respond quickly.

The primary hazard during the aerotow is getting too high above the tow plane. The glider can get high enough to lift the tail of the tow plane and cause a dive toward the ground.

> **IF THE GLIDER EVER GETS SO HIGH THE PILOT**
> **LOSES SIGHT OF THE TOW PLANE,**
> **THE PILOT MUST RELEASE AT ONCE!**

During initial flight training, the instructor will be watching you very closely. If you allow the glider to become dangerously high, the instructor will say something, or in some cases take control of the glider. If you get so high that you are not sure if you should release, quickly convey your concern to the instructor, and let the instructor help with the decision to release or not. In some cases the instructor will take control and place the glider back into normal tow position instead of releasing.

The secret to performing a satisfactory aerotow is concentration. Watch the tow plane closely and try to anticipate and react to any necessary control movements as early as possible.

THE RELEASE

When you reach the release altitude, simply look to the left and right to be sure no one is flying nearby (this is called clearing the area) then pull the release with your left hand. You will hear the release, but watch the tow rope to ensure it is disengaged before performing a gentle level turn to the right. Do not climb after release.

There is no requirement to turn any certain number of degrees after release. After you have a safe separation distance, you may turn any direction.

The tow plane always turns left after release to give separation between the glider and the tow plane.

RUNNING THE WING

There will be times when you help someone launch by running their wing. Do not hook up the tow rope to the glider until the pilot has completed the cockpit checklist. While waiting for the pilot to complete the cockpit checklist, be alert to other traffic and potential hazards such as people, parked gliders or other objects too close to the tow plane and glider takeoff path.

Show the end of the rope to the pilot for inspection of the rope for condition. Attach the tow ring to the glider release mechanism and give a jiggle to see and hear there is freedom of movement. If the ring is tight in the mechanism, it may be the wrong type of ring, or not installed properly, or there may be damage of the mechanism or rings.

After the tow rope is attached to the glider, give it a good strong tug, then walk to the wing tip of the glider. (If the glider pilot has not performed a release check, it may be necessary to try the release with a load on the rope.) When walking to the wing tip, stay well in front of the wing in case the tow plane pulls the glider forward. The wing could trip you, causing you to fall on the wing.

On your way to the wing tip, look at the canopy to see it is locked. Inspect the dive brakes to see they are locked. If the glider is equipped with flaps; are they in a logical position? Has the tail dolly been removed? These items are the responsibility of the pilot, but an alert wing runner can sometimes help prevent a pilot error that could cause an accident.

Continuously watch for conflicting air traffic. Wait for the glider pilot to give the signal to proceed with the launch, and then give the "take-up slack" signal. When the slack is removed from the tow rope, give the "stop" signal. Check once more for landing traffic, receive final confirmation the pilot is ready to launch, (usually a waggle of the glider's rudder) and give the "go" signal.

In most conditions, you need to support the wing tip for just a few strides before letting go of the wing tip. In any case, be sure not to grip the wing tip, or hold onto it too long. If you do, you may cause the glider to swerve, or ground loop. Accidents have been caused by wing runners holding onto the wing too long. When running the wing, hold the trailing edge of the wing tip between two fingers. This will help to prevent you from holding on too tight.

Sometimes the pilot will hold aileron pressure to one side while you are running the wing. You will feel pressure as the glider begins to move through the air. If you resist this pressure and then release the wing tip, the wing will suddenly tilt, perhaps contacting the ground and causing a groundloop. If you feel pressure while running the wing, it is better to allow the wing to begin to tilt while you still have hold of it. The pilot will probably feel the wing tilting and remove the aileron pressure causing this undesirable action.

FORWARD STALLS

To understand stalls, we must again look at the airfoil and angle of attack. An airfoil is curved on top so the air flowing over the top has a greater distance to travel.

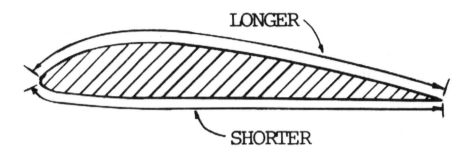

LONGER

SHORTER

The air flowing over the top only creates lift if it flows smoothly over the airfoil. If the angle of attack becomes too great, the airflow can no longer make the increasingly sharp curvature and finally begins to break away from the airfoil, destroying much of the lift. When this happens on any part of the wing, a stall has begun.

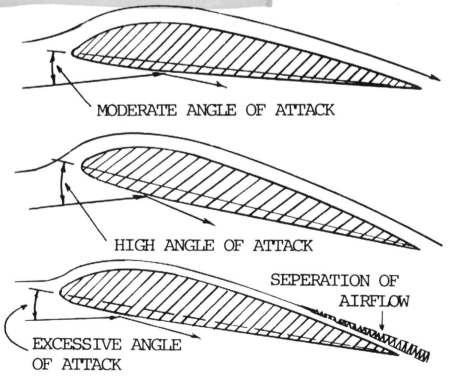

MODERATE ANGLE OF ATTACK

HIGH ANGLE OF ATTACK

SEPERATION OF AIRFLOW

EXCESSIVE ANGLE OF ATTACK

By definition, a stall occurs when the wing exceeds its critical angle of attack. The critical angle of attack of a typical airfoil is 16 - 18 degrees.

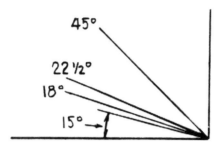

The stall is solely a function of angle of attack, not airspeed or attitude. An aircraft can be in a stalled condition at any airspeed and at any attitude. Aerobatic pilots purposely do this when they do vertical 'snap rolls' and other aerobatic maneuvers.

STALL SPEED

The solo stalling speed of a typical training glider may be listed in the flight manual as 35 knots. Several factors will cause the stall to occur at higher speeds.

1. Weight. The heavier the glider, the more lift the wing has to generate. The heavier the glider, the higher the stall speed. For example, the same glider with two heavy people may stall at 40 knots.

2. Center of gravity. Remember the balancing act going on between the CG, lift and downward tail loads? The farther forward the CG, the greater the downward tail load required. The wing has to produce more lift to offset this additional downward tail load, so the stall speed is higher with a forward CG.

3. Turns. When an aircraft turns or pulls out of a dive, it produces centrifugal force. This same centrifugal force is what keeps water in a bucket when you swing it in a circle. In effect, centrifugal force makes the glider weigh more and thus increases its stalling speed.

4. Anything that disrupts the airflow over the wing such as dirt, bugs, frost, or raindrops will increase the stall speed. Any damage that distorts the airfoil will also increase the stall speed.

5. Dive brakes being opened disrupts the airflow and will cause an increased stall speed.

6. Turbulence, gusty air, and sloppy, uncoordinated flying can also cause an increase in stall speed.

You and your instructor should note the indicated airspeed at which the stall occurs. You might find the indicated stall speed is noticeably higher than the minimum because of the above factors or even airspeed indicator errors.

THE SIX SIGNS OF A STALL

The primary purpose of stall training is early recognition of signs of an impending stall, thus preventing accidental stalls from happening.

There are six signs of an impending stall. Remember, an aircraft can be in a stalled condition at any airspeed and any flight attitude. However, we must primarily concern ourselves with the insidious type of stall that creeps up on you if you fly the glider incorrectly.

The following are the six signs of an impending stall, the order they normally occur, and how you will perceive them. You must memorize this.

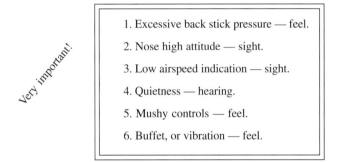

1. Excessive back stick pressure — feel.

2. Nose high attitude — sight.

3. Low airspeed indication — sight.

4. Quietness — hearing.

5. Mushy controls — feel.

6. Buffet, or vibration — feel.

Very important!

Several of your senses can warn you of a possible stall. The importance of stall practice is to develop your control response so you will make an immediate effort to stop a possible stall as soon as any one of your senses are alerted by any one or combination of the above signs.

FORWARD STALL RECOVERY

The primary purpose of stall practice is recognition of the symptoms of the stall before the stall occurs. The secondary purpose is to insure the student can make a prompt recovery from a stall with a minimum loss of height.

Since the stall occurs because of an excessive angle of attack, all we need to do to recover is to reduce the angle of attack by moving the stick forward. When we do this, the nose will move down below the horizon, the angle of attack will be reduced, the airspeed will pick up, and the wing will begin flying and producing a full amount of lift again.

Even if we did not move the stick forward, the glider would recover momentarily from a forward stall by itself! When the stall occurs, there is a loss of lift, so the glider pitches nose down (because the center of gravity is forward and the horizontal stabilizer is lifting up), picks up airspeed and begins flying again. If we held the stick back, the glider would do a series of stalls and recoveries.

If a stall occurs, your job is to make a prompt, positive recovery with a minimum loss of altitude.

To recover, lower the nose below the horizon by moving the control stick forward. Pause briefly to allow the wing to regain speed, and the angle of attack to reduce, and then ease the stick back to return to level, stable flight at a constant airspeed. During the recovery, it is very important not to bring the nose of the glider back up above the horizon in an attempt to quickly re-establish normal flying speed. You'll possibly stall again.

In fact, part of learning how to perform stalls and stall recoveries is learning how to prevent them in the first place. Most serious flying accidents are the result of stalling.

> To prevent stalls from happening, you can greatly reduce the chances of a stall by simply always flying the glider with the nose below the horizon in a proper attitude, flying at a constant, proper airspeed, and flying in a coordinated manner at all times. Keep the yaw string straight!

FURTHER CONSIDERATIONS

The stall first occurs at the trailing edge of the wing.

The ailerons are also on the trailing edge of the wing and if it weren't for something else, could stall and become ineffective before the rest of the wing. The designers want the ailerons to remain effective as long as possible, so they build a little twist to the wing so the wing tips fly at a slightly lower angle of attack than the inboard section of the wing. When the inboard section of the wing stalls, the wing tips and ailerons are still effective.

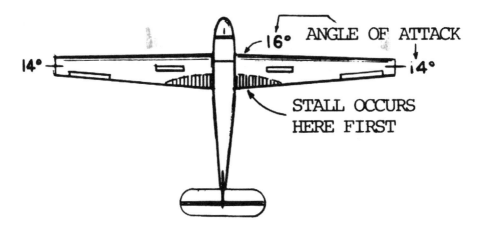

This means the stall first occurs on the trailing edge of the wing at the inboard section. As the stall progresses, the stalled area moves forward and outward on the wing. This produces a gradually increasing loss of lift, giving plenty of warning.

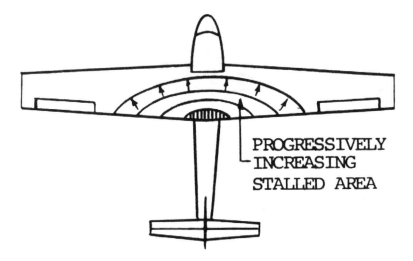

PROGRESSIVELY
INCREASING
STALLED AREA

IF A WING DROPS

When practicing forward stalls, rather than the glider pitching nose down with the wings level, you may have one wing or the other drop as the stall occurs. This can be caused by a gust, or perhaps the glider wasn't quite level as you entered the stall, or you may have been applying aileron control at the time. As the stall occurs, the stalled area favors one wing, and the glider tilts or banks to one side as the stall begins.

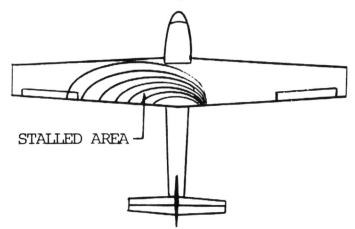

STALLED AREA

If you try to pick up a stalled, or stalling wing with the ailerons, you will make matters worse. This is because lowering the aileron has the effect of increasing the angle of attack of the wing that is already stalled. (See page 25).

Very important

IF A WING DROPS AT OR NEAR A STALL, YOU
MUST PICK IT UP WITH OPPOSITE RUDDER.

Applying opposite rudder will yaw the glider and swing the stalled wing forward. This increases the airflow over the stalled wing, reduces angle of attack, and helps produce lift and fly again.

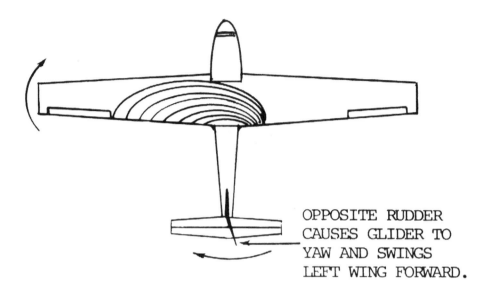

OPPOSITE RUDDER CAUSES GLIDER TO YAW AND SWINGS LEFT WING FORWARD.

The problem with this theory is under almost all other circumstances, if the wing begins to go down, the proper response is to apply opposite <u>aileron</u> to pick it back up again. Only if you are near a stall will the glider respond in a negative or even dangerous way when you apply opposite aileron.

During flight training, you will learn the proper response to a stalled wing. It is hoped years later, when a wing begins to go down and your instinctive response to apply opposite aileron doesn't work; in fact makes matters worse, you will remember this lesson and get off the opposite aileron and apply the proper opposite rudder to effect a prompt, positive recovery with a minimum loss of altitude!

EFFECT OF REDUCED 'G'

As you recover from the stall, you will feel yourself becoming lighter and will feel a funny sensation in your stomach. This is a reduced 'G' sensation and is not a sign of an impending stall.

A 'G' is one gravity. As you sit there reading this book, you are experiencing one 'G'. Riding a roller coaster, you experience higher 'G' forces at the bottom of the dips and reduced 'G' forces as the machine goes over the top of the hills.

Your instructor will demonstrate the sensation so you will have a feel for it (pun intended). Reduced 'G' forces will occur any time you move the stick forward and sometimes while flying in gusty air. You must understand this feeling is NOT a sign of a stall.

PRACTICING FORWARD, IMMINENT STALLS

Imminent stalls are very gentle stalls. Deeper, more severe stalls will be practiced later in the flight training program.

To perform an imminent stall, first establish a steady pitch attitude that will give an airspeed of 45-50 knots. Then gently raise the nose of the glider up to, or slightly above the horizon with the elevator. Recite aloud the six signs of the stall as they occur. You have to know the six signs very well, and also know the exact order they occur to say them all before the last one, the buffet, occurs.

> 1. Excessive back stick pressure — feel.
>
> 2. Nose high attitude — sight.
>
> 3. Low airspeed indication — sight.
>
> 4. Quietness — hearing.
>
> 5. Mushy controls — feel.
>
> 6. Buffet, or vibration — feel.

As soon as the first sign of a buffet is perceived, perform a recovery. Lower the nose of the glider below the horizon with the elevator. Pick up a wing that begins to drop by applying opposite rudder. Pause long enough for the glider to regain its angle of attack and flying speed, and finally, raise the nose back to the original nose-below-the-horizon attitude.

When practicing forward stall recoveries, it is important not to bring the nose of the glider back above the horizon in order to regain the entry airspeed. Only bring the nose up to the original nose-below-the horizon attitude, and wait for any excessive airspeed to dissipate.

The manner in which this stall is practiced, simulates how most stalls will likely occur by accident in real life; very gentle: slow.

An accidental stall sneaks up on you as your attention is diverted by something else. In the real world, it is hoped upon noticing any one of the six signs, you will respond and 'recover' long before all six signs occur.

DECISIONS

In all of flying, there probably is nothing more important than the knowledge and skills of this chapter. You must know and understand everything about stalls so you are able to fly safely.

WRITTEN TEST #5 - FORWARD STALLS

1. What is a stall?

2. Name 6 signs of an impending stall in the order they occur.

     a.

     b.

     c.

     d.

     e.

     f.

3. Where on the wing does a stall first occur?

4. When the wing stalls, the glider pitches nose down. Why?

5. What is the minimum stalling speed of the glider you are being trained in?

6. Can a glider stall at a higher airspeed? How?

     a.

     b.

     c.

     d.

     e.

     f.

7. Why is it important to practice stalls?

8. How is a normal recovery made from a forward stall?

9. If a wing starts to 'drop' during a forward stall, how should that wing be raised? Why?

Answers on page 151

TURNING STALLS

If a glider stalls during a turn, the inside, or down wing will tend to stall first. That's because the inside wing is traveling a shorter distance and therefore is flying at a slower airspeed and a higher angle of attack than the outside wing.

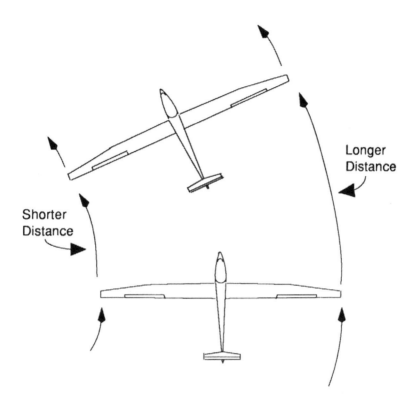

Just as in a forward stall, a turning stall occurs because the wing is at an excessive angle of attack. Unlike the forward stall, however, we have the additional problem caused by the unbalanced lift forces causing the glider to roll toward the down or (more) stalled wing. Simply reducing the angle of attack by moving the stick forward doesn't stop this inbalance and rolling motion. We can't use the aileron to stop the rolling motion because putting the stalled, inside wing's aileron down, only aggravates the stalled situation by increasing the angle of attack of that wing.

> THE FIRST STEP, THEN, TO RECOVER FROM A TURNING STALL IS TO PUSH ON THE OPPOSITE RUDDER TO STOP THE YAWING.

Opposite rudder will yaw the glider, swinging the stalled wing forward, which increases the airflow on that wing and helps the stalled wing become un-stalled. Opposite rudder also slows down the opposite, unstalled wing so it produces less lift. This helps make the whole wing produce a more balanced lifting force and stop the rolling motion.

The second step to recover from a turning stall is to move the stick forward to reduce the angle of attack of the entire wing.

Step three is very important. After the first two steps, the glider must be given time to recover from the stall. The third step is to pause so adequate flying speed is regained.

After the pause, and only then, may we use the ailerons to roll the glider level.

The step-by-step recovery procedure from a turning stall is:

1. Opposite rudder.

2. Stick forward.

3. Pause, regain flying speed.

4. Roll level with ailerons, and bring the nose to
   normal gliding attitude below the horizon.

The first two steps can be combined into one, but you must think, and say the steps in the above order. Later in your training you'll see how spin recoveries are done in the same order.

PERFORMING AN IMMINENT TURNING STALL

1. Establish a pitch attitude resulting in an airspeed of 45-50 knots.

2. Roll into a very gentle bank angle of no more than 10 degrees. (Wing tip on the horizon.)

3. Gently raise the nose of the glider just to, or slightly above the horizon.

4. Recite aloud the six signs of the stall as they occur.

5. At the moment of the buffet, effect a recovery as outlined above.

Note: At the moment of the buffet, you will be holding a slight opposite aileron pressure to prevent the wing from going down. This will slow the recovery process, so you must remove this opposite aileron pressure by bringing the stick to a neutral position.

Later on in your flight training program, during the flight test, or much later during flight checks and flight reviews by other flight instructors, you will be criticized if you are applying any opposite aileron pressure at the moment of a stall.

If a stall occurs, and a wing is low or moving to a lower position, you must resist any temptation to apply any opposite aileron control.

> Turning stalls are most likely to happen inadvertently during turns close to the ground. Rope breaks, and the 180-degree turn back to the airport, low altitude thermalling, and turns in the landing pattern are prime culprits to our safety record.

By one estimate, fully three fourths of all fatal aircraft accidents can be traced to the turning stall at low altitudes.

It is very important for you to understand it is extremely difficult, if not impossible, to stall a glider in turns of 30 degree angle of bank or more.

The reason is because in normally certificated aircraft, the elevator is built purposely to have a limited effect. In a steep turn, nearly all, if not all of the elevator's available range is used up to produce the extra lift needed in the turn. Your instructor will demonstrate this fact by having you enter a turn with a bank angle of more than 30 degrees and then having you attempt to stall the glider. Without an abrupt, violent motion of the controls, you will find it impossible to stall the glider.

In steeper turns, as the airspeed dissipates, the lift the wings are producing becomes insufficient to hold the glider up, and it begins to slide down sideways through the air, long before a stall can occur. Yaw stability causes the nose to lower much as described on page 41.

When practicing turning stalls, watch the nose of the glider. If the nose only *yaws* down through the horizon, you haven't stalled at all, and the controls still work in their normal fashion. If the glider truly stalls, the nose will *pitch* down through the horizon.

The difference between stalling and falling is, in the one case, the controls continue to work in a normal fashion, and so your natural, instinctive reactions will be correct. In the other, your instinctive reactions will be incorrect and the situation can become much worse. In both cases altitude is lost.

It's an amazing fact that from the standpoint of stalls, steep turns are safer than shallow ones. During your training, you will practice making gentle banked turning stalls. You will see even the docile trainer is much easier to stall and reacts more violently in this configuration.

WARNING: During windy conditions, or days with strong thermal activity, there is often severe turbulence, wind shear, or a high wind gradient from ground level to several hundred feet. It can be very dangerous to be turning in this turbulent zone. The need for steep turns close to the ground should be avoided, especially in windy or turbulent conditions.

To prevent turning stalls, learn to make well coordinated turns at a constant, proper airspeed. Keep the nose of the glider below the horizon and the yaw string straight!

DECISIONS

Strict aeronautical theory states an aircraft can be stalled in any attitude and any airspeed. Although this is true in the strictest sense, it is also true if the pilot flies with the nose of the glider below the horizon, and keeps the yaw string straight, it is nearly impossible to stall a normal, type certificated glider.

In straight, wings level flight, the elevator has its full effect. As soon as the glider is banked, the ability of the elevator to cause the wing to achieve a stalling angle of attack reduces so in a 30 degree angle of bank, it is nearly impossible to stall a glider.

Armed with these facts, and basic skills, a glider pilot should be safe from stalling accidents. Make the decision to become skillful at airspeed control; be alert to always keeping the nose of the glider below the horizon; keep the yaw string straight especially during turns at low altitude, and with an instructor, try stalling the glider from well banked turns, and with the nose of the glider below the horizon to convince yourself of these basic facts.

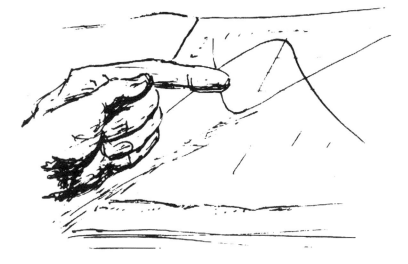

WRITTEN TEST #6 TURNING STALLS

1. Turning stalls are most likely to occur close to the ground. Why?

2. Name the three occasions when a turning stall is most likely to happen?

3. Without an abrupt control motion, a turning stall is most easily entered from a:

a. shallow turn

b. medium turn

c. steep turn

4. Give a step-by-step recovery procedure from a turning stall.

5. How do you prevent turning stalls close to the ground?

6. What is one control not to use during the first steps of a turning stall recovery?

7. From the standpoint of turning stalls, the most difficult angle of bank to stall a glider is:

a. shallow turn

b. medium turn

c. steep turn

Answers on page 152

FLIGHT AT CRITICALLY SLOW SPEEDS
(INCIPIENT STALLS)

During the flight test you will be asked to fly the glider at a speed just above minimum stall speed. The examiner will be watching to see if you understand the problems of slow speeds and high angles of attack.

High angles of attack are the key words. At very slow speeds, you are flying very close to the critical angle of attack. Any increase of the angle of attack will cause a stall to occur with resulting loss to lift. In addition, any increase in weight or *wing loading* will also cause a stall. (Wing loading is the amount of weight per square foot the wing is supporting).

During critically slow airspeeds, the controls are not very effective, and any course, overuse of any of the controls may cause a stall. You will be holding the control stick well aftto maintain the high angle of attack necessary for the slow speed. You must be careful not to move the stick back any further. One useful hint is to use the horizon as an attitude indicator to maintain a steady airspeed/angle of attack, and only glance at the airspeed indicator from time to time to verify you are flying at the selected airspeed.

If a gust causes a wing to begin to bank (glider to roll) while you are trying to hold a straight glide at a critically slow speed, you may not be able to roll the wings back level by using opposite aileron without stalling.

Remember, the ailerons work by changing angle of attack. If you try to pick up a stalling/falling wing with ailerons, you will be increasing the angle of attack of a wing that is already at, or near, its critical angle of attack, and that wing may stall.

As you build your flying hours you will develop certain habits. Many of your habit patterns will become nearly instinctive. One of these instinctive reactions will cause you to attempt to pick up a dropping wing with opposite aileron, and coordinated application of rudder. More than 99 percent of the time this will be the correct reaction. But, during flight at critically slow airspeeds, if you react in the usual manner, you may cause one wing to stall. This can result in a spin. When flying at very high angles of attack, you need to develop different skills and perceptions to make you think and fly differently than you do while flying at higher speeds. Your mind has to 'shift gears' to keep you from making mistakes.

To correct for a dropping wing during flight at a critically slow airspeed, you must use opposite rudder. Let's suppose the left wing is going down. At critically slow airspeeds when one wing drops, you must assume it is stalled. There are actually two problems . . . first, one wing isn't producing enough lift (the left one in our example) and second, the other wing is producing too much lift.

Attempting to use the ailerons will only aggravate the situation. Opposite aileron usage will lower the left aileron in our example, causing an increased angle of attack on the portion of the wing that is already at, or near, its critical angle of attack. But opposite rudder, (right rudder) will cause the glider to yaw, swinging the stalled wing forward, increasing its relative airspeed and decreasing its angle of attack so it becomes un-stalled, producing more lift and raising the wing. The right wing in our example is still producing lift (too much lift) and is slowed down when opposite rudder is used, so that it produces less lift which lowers that wing.

So, at critically slow airspeeds, you must remember to keep the wings level and/or correct for a dropping wing by using opposite rudder.

During the flight test, you will be asked to perform different turns while flying at critically slow airspeeds. Remember, an aircraft gains weight due to centrifugal force in a turn, so the wing loading increases. During critically slow airspeeds you must use very gentle bank angles. If you want to make a quicker rate of turn necessitating a steeper angle of bank, you need to increase the airspeed.

The uninformed person believes the rudder turns an aircraft. As a matter of fact, all of us at one time thought the rudder turns the aircraft. We have nearly an instinctive intuition about mechanical things which helps us figure out how things work. Unfortunately, we are not always correct. This is especially true of our mistaken belief that a rudder turns an aircraft. (You probably think a rudder turns a boat too. This is another example of incorrect reasoning. I'll let you discover for yourself why a boat turns).

This misconception of the rudder function causes most pilots to use excessive rudder during turns Especially turns when the pilot is under stress. It has been said the majority of all fatal aircraft accidents are the result of the pilot using excessive rudder in the direction of the turn.

Doing this while at a critically slow airspeed can cause the lowered wing to slow down below the critical airspeed and stall. Thus, the incorrect reactions of a pilot must be suppressed and new reactions developed by thorough training and practice.

How much rudder is enough? How much is too much? These questions are easily answered. While making any turn . . . use as much rudder as necessary to keep the yaw string straight. As amazing as it may seem, we could eliminate one of the major causes of all fatal aircraft accidents by simply keeping the yaw string straight with judicious use of the rudder.

This is especially true during flights at critically slow airspeeds and during any turns close to the ground such as: the landing pattern, low altitude thermalling and low altitude emergencies such as rope breaks.

During your flight test, the examiner will watch closely how you react should a wing begin to bank while at critically slow speeds. Don't use opposite aileron. Use opposite rudder.

The examiner will also watch how you make all other turns. Be careful not to use excessive rudder. Keep the yaw string straight.

Finally, the examiner will watch how you control the airspeed. Don't stare at the airspeed indicator, watch the horizon and hold a constant pitch attitude (relative position of the nose below the horizon) to maintain a steady speed.

THERMALLING TECHNIQUE

The ability to soar, means the ability to stay aloft. There are several forms of lifting air currents in the atmosphere. The most common is thermal lift. Thermals can be thought of as columns of warm air created by the sun heating the surface of the earth. Sailplanes and soaring birds are often seen to circle silently within the boundaries of the column of lift and are seen to rise almost effortlessly.

The ability to find and use this form of lift is the basic skill you will develop in order to enjoy the thrills of soaring flight.

A thermal is usually an invisible column of rising air. Sometimes it is revealed as a column of spinning, whirling dust rising off the ground, or sometimes leaves, newspapers and cornstalks give evidence of the solar-powered energy source. Gliding through the air, you will encounter turbulence caused by the instability of the air, and sometimes feel a surge of lift as the sailplane rises against you as it encounters a thermal. The variometer is the instrument showing if the sailplane is rising or sinking, and, realizing you are climbing, you begin a gentle turn.

A beginner often turns too soon when lift is encountered. This causes the glider to immediately leave the thermal. Thinking a turn was made in the wrong direction, the pilot then tries a turn in the opposite direction. No lift is found in this direction and logically, the pilot assumes it was only a small bump rather than a real thermal. Several minutes and several bumps later, the pilot is sitting on the ground while others are still aloft.

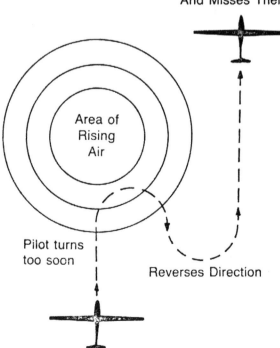

And Misses Thermal

Area of Rising Air

Pilot turns too soon

Reverses Direction

✱ It's important to fly well into the thermal before making the first turn. Wait a minimum of three seconds (five seconds is often better) after encountering lift before beginning the turn.

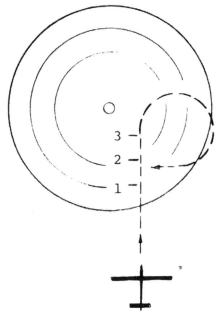

WHICH WAY TO TURN

If another sailplane is circling in the thermal you are joining, you must circle in the same direction. It makes no difference if the other sailplane is higher or lower than you. With experience, you will learn how to read evidence in cumulus clouds to help you decide just where to go and which direction to turn.

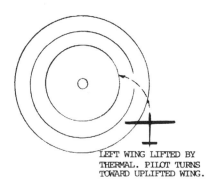

LEFT WING LIFTED BY THERMAL. PILOT TURNS TOWARD UPLIFTED WING.

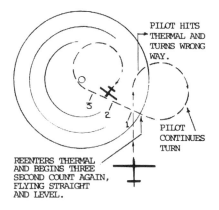

PILOT HITS THERMAL AND TURNS WRONG WAY.

PILOT CONTINUES TURN

REENTERS THERMAL AND BEGINS THREE SECOND COUNT AGAIN, FLYING STRAIGHT AND LEVEL.

It is important to continue circling in the same direction once you have begun to thermal. It is very difficult to form an idea of what exact shape a thermal is. (They are seldom round.) Attempts at reversing the thermalling direction usually finds the glider pilot "lost" trying to relocate the center, or "core," of the thermal.

CENTERING

A thermal usually has a core of stronger lift. For the best rate of climb, you should position the glider in this core. This is done by flying straight and level for three seconds whenever you encounter stronger lift, then resuming the turn. A series of adjustments such as this will guide the sailplane to the core.

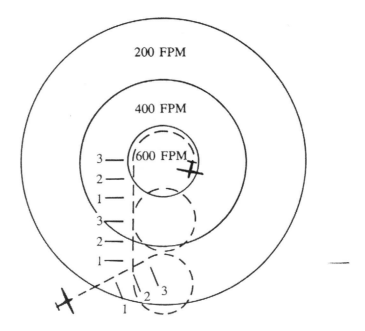

BANK ANGLE AND AIRSPEED

A sailplane's minimum sink rate occurs when it is flying straight and level. As the craft begins a turn, centrifugal force makes it weigh more, and the sink rate increases. The steeper the bank angle, the higher the sink rate. For this reason, you don't want to bank the glider any steeper than necessary to stay in the best part of the thermal. It is seldom necessary to use a bank angle of more than forty-five degrees to remain in the core of most thermals. Steeper angles of bank are used when the thermal is small. Thermals expand as they gain altitude, so a glider pilot would use shallower bank angles at higher altitudes. A thirty-degree angle of bank is probably the most often used by pilots while thermalling.

Proper thermalling airspeed will usually be several miles per hour or knots above stall speed. The flight manual will indicate the minimum sinking speed for the glider. This minimum sinking speed occurs in straight and level flight, at the minimum flying weight. Minimum sinking speed increases if the flying weight is above the minimum allowable, and as the bank angle is increased. Typical sailplanes climb best using 45 to 50 knots airspeed. If the thermal is turbulent, a faster airspeed will be desirable for better control of the glider. It is not unusual for a heavy sailplane to thermal at 60 knots. (One knot equals 1.15 m.p.h.. 60 knots = 69 m.p.h..)

You should develop the ability to fly round circles using a constant angle of bank and a constant airspeed for efficient thermalling. Thermals are abstract objects and the best way to deal with an unknown is to form a base you know is true, and work from that base. The "base" when dealing with an abstract thermal is a round circle which you are able to shift around until you find the core.

SAFETY

As a student pilot, you should not attempt thermalling at low altitudes or near the airport traffic pattern. One thousand feet above ground level (AGL) is a reasonable minimum thermalling altitude for student pilots in most situations. Circumstances at your airport may make it necessary to raise this minimum. Ask your instructor for guidance on this matter.

If you are below 1,000 feet and find a thermal, you should land, explain to the tow pilot where the thermal was, and ask to be taken there at a safe altitude on the next aero tow.

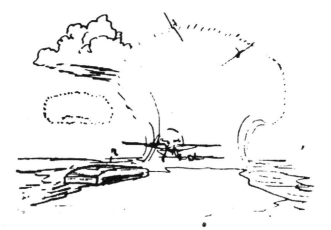

SLACK ROPE

Slack in the tow rope can only occur when the glider has a faster speed than the tow plane. This could happen if the tow plane slows down suddenly, but this is not very likely.

The most common time to have slack in the tow rope is during, and especially after turns. If the glider pilot permits the glider to be incorrectly outside the circular arc of the path of the tow plane, the glider is then on a larger arc. Since the glider is flying a greater distance, it must fly a faster airspeed.

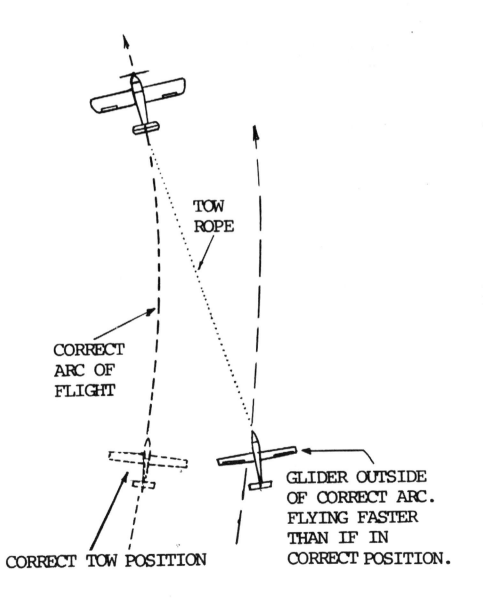

TOW
ROPE

CORRECT
ARC OF
FLIGHT

CORRECT TOW POSITION

GLIDER OUTSIDE
OF CORRECT ARC.
FLYING FASTER
THAN IF IN
CORRECT POSITION.

The tow rope won't go slack at this time unless the glider pilot suddenly moves in towards the correct position. If you ever find yourself in this position, you will need to move back very gently with perhaps some small application of dive brakes for increased drag. Dive brakes would only be used in extreme situations.

The most likely time for slack to occur is when the glider is outside the turn as described, and then the tow plane straightens out to fly stright. This will leave the tow plane and glider flying at different speeds, so the glider will catch up and slack will form.

It is also possible for the glider pilot to allow the glider to rise to an extremely high position during tow, and, in attempting to get back down to the correct tow position, cause slack in the tow rope.

You will best prevent slack from forming by maintaining a correct tow position.

Another possibility of slack forming is during turbulence. It isn't likely you will fly during very turbulent conditions in your pre-solo training program.

GETTING RID OF SLACK

Modern tow rope is very shock absorbing without being springy. For this reason it isn't likely you will encounter severe slack in the rope. Minor slack doesn't need any particular response.

Moderate slack should be removed by first doing nothing. The tow plane will speed up slightly when the slack forms and will take up the slack itself. You should simply assume, and hold the correct tow position.

If the rope is allowed to come tight with a hard jerk, the rope might break. To help soften the jerk, the glider pilot should yaw the glider away from the rope with the rudder just before the rope comes tight. When the rope does come tight, it will pull the nose of the glider around which helps absorb the shock.

If you yaw the glider too early, or apply dive brakes while maintaining position, you will cause the glider to slow down which causes a greater speed differential between the tow plane and glider and more likely break the rope.

Another method is to lower the nose of the glider a moment before the rope becomes tight to accelerate the glider to approximate the tow plane's speed. This technique requires more piloting skill.

If the slack is severe, it may be best to release the rope to prevent any possibility of the rope fouling on the glider.

PATTERN ENTRY

Landings are a three dimensional problem. You must learn to deal with height, distance, and time in order to land the glider at a desired place. Also, you must be able to fly within airspace often occupied by other aircraft with the same intention of landing.

Every airport has organized landing patterns, which aircraft join and fly in a prescribed manner. The standard landing pattern uses left hand turns, and thus is called a left hand landing pattern.

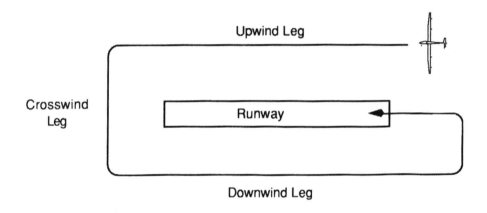

Some airport runways have a conflict with terrain features or perhaps buildings such as hospitals and schools, which dictate a different, right hand landing pattern. If an airport uses a non-standard (right hand) landing pattern for one or more runways, a landing direction indicator will indicate which direction to use. The landing direction indicator is a segmented circle with a wind direction indicator in the center, and traffic pattern indicators representing the landing direction for the different runways.

(see drawing on next page)

The basic landing pattern is a 360-degree landing pattern. It is so named because of the four, 90 degree turns - equaling 360 degrees. This landing pattern has four legs, which are named in reference to the wind direction, assuming a landing into the wind. A 360-degree pattern has an upwind leg, a crosswind leg, a downwind leg, a base leg and a final leg.

THE SEGMENTED CIRCLE

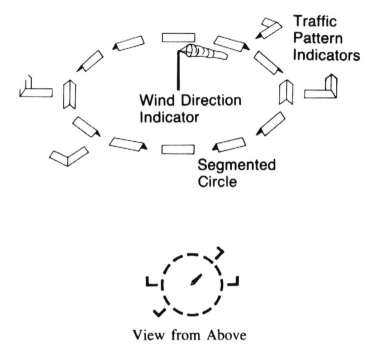

View from Above

An aircraft planning to land at an airport is expected to join the landing pattern at a forty-five degree angle so as to afford the best visibility of other possible aircraft in the traffic pattern to both the pilot of the joining aircraft and those pilots of aircraft already in the pattern.

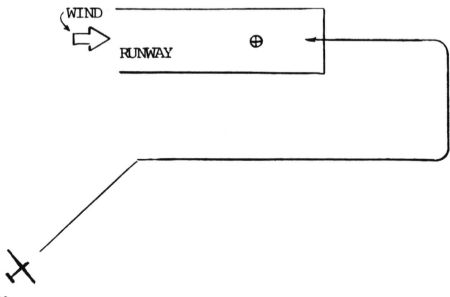

A pilot may be joining the traffic pattern from any of several directions. It is permitted to join the landing pattern at any point of the landing pattern. In so doing, a pilot may eliminate any or several of the legs of the standard landing pattern. Thus, a pilot may perform a 360 degree pattern (four 90 degree turns), a 270 degree pattern (three 90 degree turns), a 180-degree pattern with only two 90 degree turns, a 90 degree pattern with only one 90 degree turn, or even a straight-in approach with no turns at all.

The most desirable landing pattern is a full, 360-degree landing pattern. The least desirable is the straight in approach. In the case of gliders, it is important to plan the flight so as to be able to perform a full landing pattern. Without an engine, a glider only has one chance to perform a safe landing. A full 360 pattern affords the glider pilot full opportunity to inspect the landing site (especially off-field landings) for obstructions, wind direction, slope, and in the case of an off-field landing, livestock. A 360 pattern allows the glider pilot to make adjustments in the pattern to account for unexpected sinking air.

It is acceptable practice to fly directly over the center of the airport, and join the downwind leg. This is called an overhead approach and should only be used at an airport with no other possible conflicting traffic.

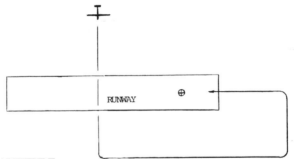

PATTERN ALTITUDE

A normal landing pattern altitude for piston driven aircraft can be anywhere from 600 feet above ground level (AGL) to 1,500 AGL. The standard height if there are no other published heights for a specific airport is 1,000 feet above ground level.

If the glider pilot is flying at an airport with other power aircraft, it will be best to conform to the power traffic rules. However, glider pilots need to develop skills necessary to make safe landings in farmer's fields where there may be obstructions, slopes and other hazards. The altitude of the farmer's field above sea level will probably be unknown, so the pilot will have to use visual clues, and learn how to judge heights without the use of the altimeter.

Pilots use three references when making judgments about height. First there are the relative sizes of familiar things. As you go higher, houses, and cows appear to become smaller.

Second, are angles to a point on the ground. Objects seen at a low angle to the horizon are far away and hard to get to, and objects observed at a steep downward angle are close.

Finally, we use depth perception. Depth perception works on the basis of binocular vision. Your two eyes send a signal to your brain, and your brain computes the angular difference between the two eyes to give you three-dimensional vision from which distances can be judged.

Binocular vision is very limited in accuracy as you get farther away from an object. In fact, at distances further than 500 feet, the accuracy in which distances can be judged will be off an average of 30%. For this reason, the best height for a glider pilot to fly a landing pattern will permit the glider pilot to be at 500 feet AGL (Above Ground Level) opposite the touch down point on the downwind leg. This permits a safe height to perform the remaining pattern and turns, while providing maximum use of all judgmental faculties. If there is a strong wind, or expected turbulence, this altitude must be raised for safety.

A word about altimeters. The altimeter is the least reliable of all the instruments. One of the reasons for this is a human must set it. The altimeter is adjusted before each flight with a knob located on the lower left corner. Logically thinking, you would believe if you wanted the hands to rotate clockwise, you would rotate the knob clockwise as you do a wristwatch. Not so! Rotating the knob clockwise turns the hands counter-clockwise! Also, reading the three hands to obtain a correct altitude isn't easy. During a flying career, every pilot will set the altimeter incorrectly, and will interpret the reading incorrectly. Many accidents can be attributed to the pilot believing an altimeter that was giving incorrect information.

It is important to develop the attitude never to trust the altimeter. Learn to fly the landing pattern accurately and safely without using the altimeter.

While flying on the upwind leg of the 360-degree pattern, a glider pilot may encounter unusual lifting or sinking air. If lift is encountered, the pilot can deploy the dive brakes to continue the optimum sink rate, or perhaps continue the upwind leg. If unusual sinking air is encountered, the glider pilot must turn onto the crosswind leg early.

This same technique is used while on the crosswind leg.

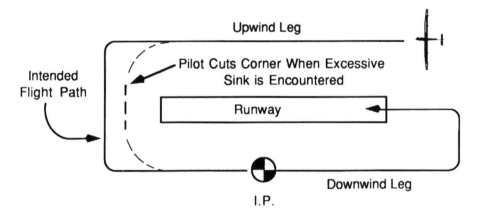

The object is to arrive at the I.P. (Initial Point) at the planned altitude. It is very important not to arrive at the I.P. lower than planned. It is normal to approach the I.P. a little high, so the glider pilot always needs to use some dive brake to get down to the I.P. height.

It is not possible to accurately arrive at the I.P. time and again without using dive brakes. The whole object of the landing pattern is to fly at a height always a little too high, and lose the excess height with the use of the dive brakes.

If the pilot ever allows the glider to be too low, there is little that can be done to fly a normal landing pattern. For this reason, the pilot must always fly the landing pattern a little higher than absolutely necessary and spoil off the excess altitude with the dive brakes.

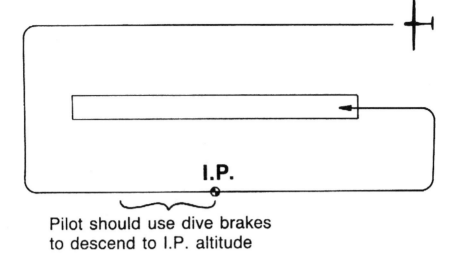

Pilot should use dive brakes
to descend to I.P. altitude

If it should happen you are lower than intended during the landing pattern, you must assume if this continues, you will have to adjust the landing pattern so as to perform a safe landing. This will often mean you will not be able to land at the intended point.

Safety is the most important criterion. If you land at the intended point using a non-standard or unsafe landing approach, or worse, if you have an accident because you insist on proceeding with the original landing pattern without enough height and speed, the Federal Aviation Agency or the operators of the airport or club may punish you.

On the other hand, if you find you must land at other than the intended point because of unusual conditions or faulty judgment, and then display good judgment by flying a safe landing pattern to a safe, proper landing to a different point, you will be judged as a mature, safe pilot.

Because we fly in an invisible air mass, it is impossible to predict when we may encounter strong downdrafts during the landing pattern. Sooner or later, every pilot will have the situation arise when a normal landing pattern is not possible. In most cases the pilot will have to turn onto base leg early and land well along the runway. In some rare, unusually severe cases, pilots had to land on a different runway.

Safely lands well down runway

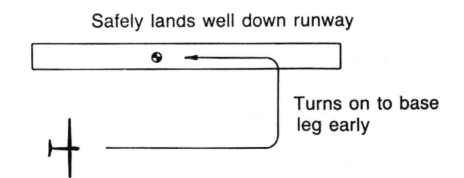

Turns on to base
leg early

Pilot too low to perform normal landing pattern

LANDINGS

(The TLAR, or "That Looks About Right" technique)

To understand how and why we fly the landing pattern as we do, we look at the landing pattern backwards. That is, we will first look at the final leg, then the base leg and then the downwind leg.

One of the ways the performance of a sailplane is measured is how far it can glide from a given height. This is expressed as the *glide ratio*. The glide ratio of modern sailplanes ranges from about 20-to-1 to over 60-to-1. A sailplane having a 34-to-1 (usually expressed 34:1) would be able to glide 34 miles in still air if it began from an altitude of one mile.

While flying the landing pattern, a pilot purposely flies a little too high all the way around the landing pattern. The pilot then uses spoilers or dive brakes to decrease the glide ratio and lose altitude more rapidly. In this fashion, excess altitude is "spoiled off" and the pilot is able to touch down on the runway with amazing precision.

THE LANDING CONE

When the glider enters the final leg, it must be above it's shallowest glide slope (maximum glide ratio). (drawings not to scale)

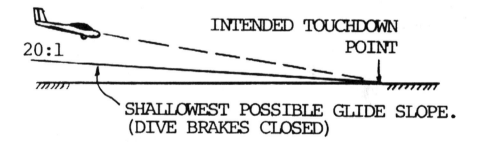

If the pilot allows the glider to be below the shallowest glide slope, it will not make it to the intended touchdown point. It will land short.

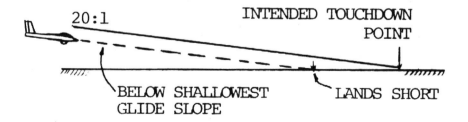

The typical glide slope when dive brakes are fully opened is about 5-to-1 for modern sailplanes. This allows the glider to descend at the steepest possible glide slope.

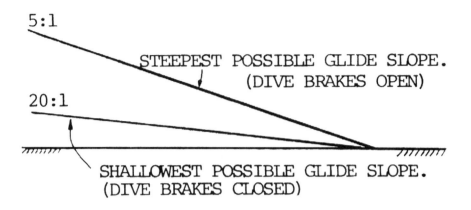

5:1

STEEPEST POSSIBLE GLIDE SLOPE.
(DIVE BRAKES OPEN)

20:1

SHALLOWEST POSSIBLE GLIDE SLOPE.
(DIVE BRAKES CLOSED)

If the pilot enters the final leg above the glider's steepest glide slope, it will land beyond the intended touchdown point.

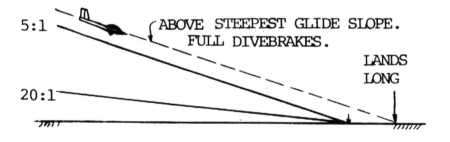

5:1

ABOVE STEEPEST GLIDE SLOPE.
FULL DIVEBRAKES.

LANDS
LONG

20:1

(A pilot can further reduce the minimum glide ratio by side-slipping the glider. This will be covered in a future lesson.)

There is a "cone" between the steepest possible glide slope (dive brakes open) and the shallowest possible glide slope (dive brakes closed). The pilot must fly the landing pattern so as to be within this cone when the glider arrives on the final leg. An ideal location would be halfway between the glider's maximum and minimum glide slope with the dive brakes approximately half opened. (In calm air.)

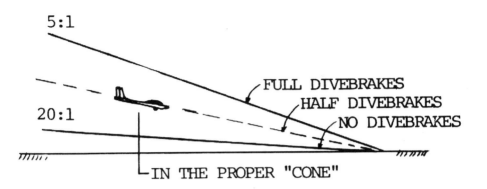

Being able to recognize these glide slopes or angles becomes the crux of the judgment problem for beginning students. You will learn this judgment by repetition of correct landing patterns, with your instructor's help.

LEARNING GLIDE ANGLES

The important glide ratios (angles) of 5:1, 12:1 and 20:1 can be easily demonstrated.

First you must understand when we speak of glide ratios of say 5:1, we mean 5 of anything versus 1 of the same thing. (We are actually referring to the distance traveled versus the height required to obtain that distance.)

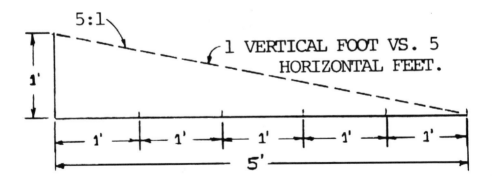

We could use 5 feet versus 1 foot.

Or, we could use 5 people heights versus 1 person height.

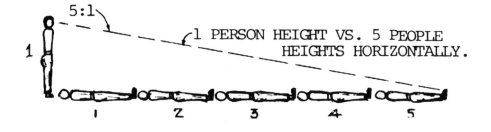

5:1

1

1 PERSON HEIGHT VS. 5 PEOPLE
HEIGHTS HORIZONTALLY.

1   2   3   4   5

One of your heights is equal to about two of your full paces. Therefore, in order to simulate a 5:1 glide slope, you simply need to step off 10 paces and then look back to your starting point. (A pace is a long step.)

Find three markers. Go outside and place one marker on the ground, then step off ten paces from this marker. Turn around and look back to the first marker. The first marker represents the touch down point. You are looking at a 5:1 glide slope. The glide slope with the dive brakes fully opened. This is the steepest the glider will come down in still air.

It is best if you face sideways to look at the marker. Psychologists tell us we can perceive angles better from our side, and this is the way you'll be looking at the touch down point just after you turn onto the base leg. Point to the marker with your outstretched arm. Learn this important angle.

How you perceive this angle is a personal thing. Some people see this for the first time and say, "Wow, that's steep!" While others say, "Wow that's shallow!"

Place a second marker on the ground at the 5:1 spot where you are standing, then step off an additional 14 paces. (10 + 14 = 24 paces divided by 2 equals 12.) This new point represents a 12:1 glide slope. When you look back at the first marker, you are seeing a 12:1 angle. (Half way between 5 and 20)

Now place the third marker where you are standing and step off 16 more paces to simulate a 20:1 glide slope. (10 + 14 + 16 = 40 divided by 2 = 20:1.)

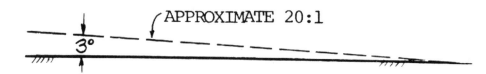

APPROXIMATE 20:1

3°

As long as the glider pilot enters the final leg somewhere between the easily recognizable cone of 5:1 to 20:1, the glider will be able to glide to the touch down point with the help of the dive brakes, assuming calm air.

If there is a headwind to fly into during the final leg, the glider pilot must be higher than if there was no wind. For this reason, glider pilots should plan their landing pattern so as to be in the upper limit of the landing cone. The zone between 5:1 and 12:1 is the most important, for this is where you want to be with almost any sailplane, in most normal conditions.

THE TURN ONTO THE BASE LEG

In order to place the glider on the final leg between the 5:1 - 20:1 cone, the pilot must turn onto the base leg at an appropriate time and position. The single, most important decision to be made during the landing pattern is where to turn into the base leg.

Let's assume three gliders with a maximum glide ratio of 20:1 enter the landing pattern at the same time and altitude...

The first one turns onto the base leg early and realizes the glider is at the top of the landing cone at the 5:1 glide angle. The pilot opens the dive brakes fully to permit the glider to land at the desired touch down point.

The second pilot turns later and finds the glider in the middle of the cone. Opening the dive brakes about half way permits the glider to descend at a 12:1 glide angle and the glider will also touch down at the intended point.

The third pilot turns still later and finds the glider at the 20:1 glide ratio. Because there is no wind, the pilot knows that if the dive brakes are left closed, the glider will just be able to make it to the touch down point.

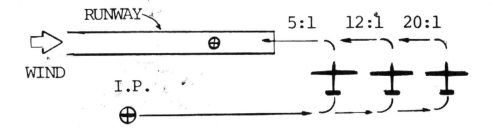

As can be seen in the above drawing, the precise spot the pilot turns onto the base leg is therefore, not a critical one. There is a large area where the turn can be made and still be within the proper cone. The only important thing is not to turn onto the base leg too early or too late.

As it turns out, it is not very likely a pilot who is watching these important angles will turn onto base leg too late. As you have seen, the 20:1 angle becomes so shallow, our built-in conservative nature will usually make us turn early enough. As it turns out, this same conservative nature often causes us to turn onto the base leg too soon. We often find ourselves too high. By careful observation at your home gliderport, you will notice most pilots need to use full dive brakes during the final leg. They are at the top of the cone. You might also notice nearly all grossly incorrect landings are too long. Grossly short landings almost never occur. Pilots tend to turn onto the base leg too early.

THE DOWNWIND LEG

> The primary decision to be made during the downwind leg,
> is where to turn onto the base leg.

As mentioned before, the decision is not a critical one. Most people want to turn onto the base leg too soon.

To help you develop the judgment necessary to perform accurate landings, you will repeat several landings with your instructor's help. There are key locations along the pattern you should announce out loud.

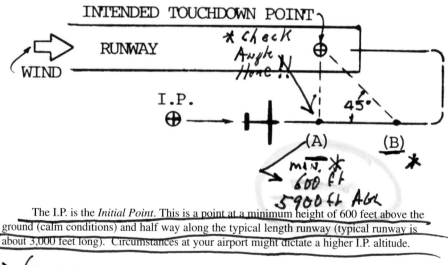

The I.P. is the *Initial Point*. This is a point at a minimum height of 600 feet above the ground (calm conditions) and half way along the typical length runway (typical runway is about 3,000 feet long). Circumstances at your airport might dictate a higher I.P. altitude.

Point "A" is a point directly opposite the touch down point.

Point "B" is a point where you are looking backward over your shoulder at the touch down point at an angle of 45 degrees.

102

The significance of point "B" is that under normal, no wind circumstances, this will be too early to turn onto the base leg.

Announcing points A and B out loud helps your instructor know you are using the system properly. Instructors have a difficult time trying to guess just what a student is thinking about.

BACK TO THE BASE LEG

After you make the turn onto the base leg you should immediately look at the angle you perceive to the touch down point. Are you below 5:1?

Your instructor will ask you, "What do you think about the angle?" and you might answer, as one of my students did, "That Looks About Right." (Thus the name for this method of teaching landings — TLAR.)

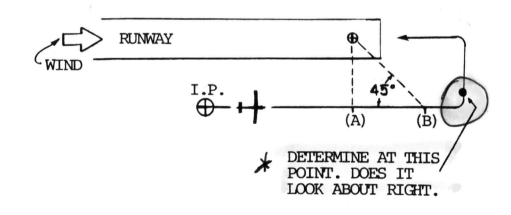

Fly The plane!!

If you turn onto base leg and it *doesn't* look right, you may turn so as to cut off part of the pattern, thus shortening the flight path, or perhaps turning away from the pattern and thus lengthening the flight path to allow more room and time to get down into the cone.

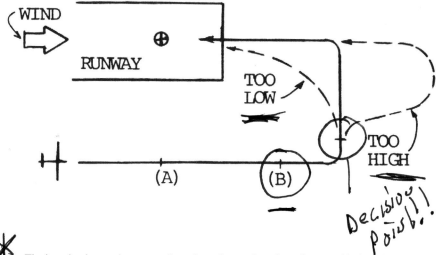

The base leg is very important. In order to have a base leg of reasonable length to allow the above adjustments, you must fly the downwind leg at a respectable distance from the runway. If the downwind leg is too close to the runway, you won't have room for a base leg and only will be able to do a 180-degree turn.

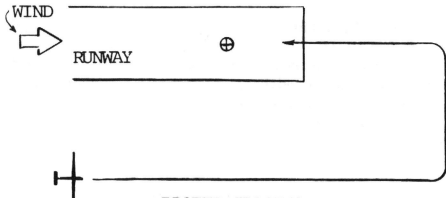

Ideally, the base leg should be long enough to permit two 90-degree turns and enough space for some maneuvering if necessary.

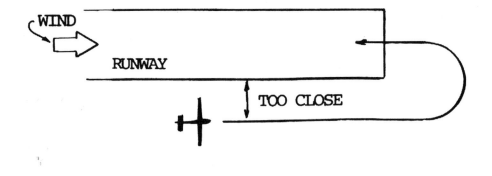

While flying along the downwind leg, you should be no closer than a 45-degree angle (looking down) to the runway. Although not critically important, a 30-degree angle would be a good angle to fly on the downwind leg.

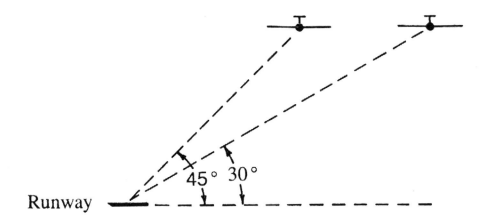

NO NO'S ON BASE LEG

As a student pilot, you should never attempt one maneuver – the buttonhook pattern.

This requires a rapid change of bank from left to right and can be a very dangerous maneuver at low altitudes. (Any turn close to the ground is a dangerous maneuver.) As a student pilot, if you realize you are high as you are about to turn onto final, you should open the dive brakes fully and land further along the runway.

Being too high on the base leg is caused by errors in judgment. It is important you do not continue to make mistakes which might lead to a bad landing or possible accident.

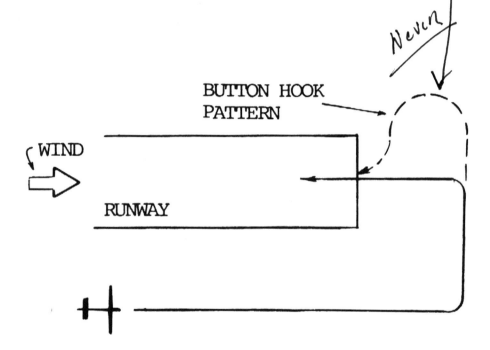

TAKE A WALK

That's the TLAR system. Before reading beyond this page, take two markers outside and walk around a simulated "landing pattern."

Take this book with you and place a marker to represent the touch down point. Start at a point that would represent the I.P., walk to a point opposite your touch down point and announce out loud "Point A." Continue to a point that is a 45-degree angle back to the touch down point and announce "Point B," continue until you think you should turn into the base leg. (Try to judge the glide angles.) Place your second marker here and make your turn onto base leg. Do the above before reading further.

Immediately make a decision: are you going to be in the cone under 5:1? Does it look about right? What glide slope does it look like? 5:1? 7:1? 10:1? 12:1? 15:1?

Note: Before reading any further it is important that you actually do the above. If it isn't convenient at this time, wait until it is before continuing your reading.

TLAR CONTINUED

You should be standing at a point of the pretend landing pattern where you have just turned onto the base leg. You have made the turn onto the base leg and have made a decision as to what angle you think you see. The actual numbers are not as important as whether you are below the 5:1 slope or not. Ideally, you should be closer to the 12:1 slope. Chances are, however, like most people, you are very close to, or even steeper than 5:1.

Pace off the distance from the second marker (where you turned onto the base leg) to the touch down marker. Divide the number of paces by 2 to determine the glide angle.

Almost everybody turns too soon on this demonstration despite all the discussion and explanation. If you didn't, give yourself a pat on the back.

If you joined the majority of students by turning very close to the 5:1 angle, remember you will do exactly the same thing in the air. This tendency to turn onto the base leg too soon is by far the most common mistake made by all pilots, regardless of experience.

ONE MORE TIME

Again, that's the TLAR system. A system based on easily learned glide slopes (or angles) to a fixed point. Once you learn the angles, you will find it safe and easy to land anywhere, be it another airport or farmer's field.

However, there is much more to a landing pattern.

Before entering the I.P. you need to check the wind direction indicator, check the pattern for other aircraft possibly landing with you, and look for other aircraft, people or vehicles on the runway.

As you enter the I.P. at 600 feet, you will complete a three-item checklist. (Later on, this checklist will be expanded.)

1. Disregard the altimeter.
2. Put your hand on the dive brake handle.
3. Establish the proper pattern airspeed.

The type of sailplane you are flying, and other factors may make it necessary to add to this basic checklist.

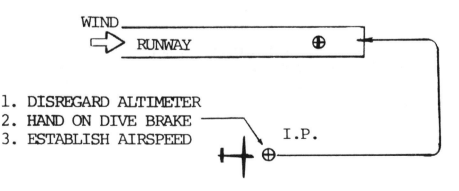

108

Disregard the altimeter after entering the I.P. Once you are in the landing pattern, you should be judging angles to decide when to turn onto the base leg, not using or watching the altimeter. The altimeter is the most error-prone instrument in the aircraft, and it's often not usable on off-field landings, so you must learn to judge angles.

Gliders are built for right-handed people. Most of the controls, such as dive brakes, flaps, landing gear, trim, etc., are on the left side of the cockpit in modern sailplanes. It is easy for a pilot to get confused and put their hand on the wrong device during the landing. Putting your hand on the dive brake handle at the I.P. and keeping it there for the remainder of the flight develops a habit, which will keep you from making a mistake later.

AIRSPEED

The proper airspeed is very important to a properly executed landing pattern. Flying too fast results in excessive energy that will have to be dissipated, and flying too slowly can be dangerous.

The proper airspeed in the landing is the sailplane's speed for maximum glide ratio, or maximum L/D (lift divided by drag), plus 1/2 of any wind, and an additional factor if it is turbulent and/or gusty.

If you don't know the speed for max L/D, you can approximate it by adding half stall speed to the glider's stall speed. Many gliders have max L/D speed near 52 knots.

Basic pattern speed (max L/D speed)	51
1/2 of today's 10 knot wind speed	_5
Today's pattern speed	56

A higher basic pattern speed might be used for possible turbulence such as encountered in dust devils. Your instructor will help you with this.

THE DOWNWIND LEG

OK, you have entered the I.P., and finished the pre-landing checklist. You will continue watching for other aircraft in the air, and for obstructions in the landing area. You must monitor the airspeed indicator every few seconds to verify you are flying a constant, correct airspeed.

Remember, you do not control the airspeed by watching the airspeed indicator. A steady, constant airspeed is best controlled by watching the horizon and keeping the nose of the glider below the horizon at a constant pitch attitude. Glance at the airspeed indicator frequently to verify you are keeping a proper pitch attitude.

The airspeed *must* remain constant throughout the landing pattern. Allowing the airspeed to change causes the apparent angles to change, making it more difficult to learn the angles and make accurate landings.

The downwind leg should be a descending flight path. The glider should always be too high, and the excess altitude spoiled off with the dive brakes.

You should be losing altitude — but not too much! As a rule of thumb, you should average 200 - 400 feet per minute or 2-4 knots (nearly the same thing) sinking rate during the downwind leg. This rule doesn't apply to the base or final legs.

During the downwind leg, monitor the variometer to verify you are descending at a proper rate. If you are not descending fast enough, open the dive brakes to help the glider attain a faster sink rate.

If you open the dive brakes and still are not going down fast enough, you will say to yourself, "I'm going through lifting air, so I'll have to modify the TLAR system and extend the downwind leg farther." (Be sure the variometer is working properly.)

On the other hand, should you encounter excessive sinking air during the downwind leg, and the variometer shows more than 400 feet per minute (4 knots) down, you will have to say, "This time I'm going down faster than normal, so if this persists, I'll have to modify the TLAR system and turn onto the base leg sooner."

Of course, while you're on the downwind leg you still announce aloud point A and point B.

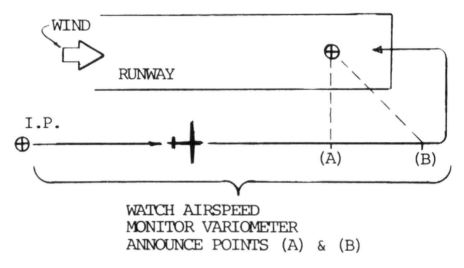

WATCH AIRSPEED
MONITOR VARIOMETER
ANNOUNCE POINTS (A) & (B)

THE TURN ONTO BASE LEG

The turn onto the base leg should be approximately a 45 degree banked turn, well coordinated, and at a constant airspeed.

Most fatal aircraft accidents occur during turns close to the ground. The safest turns are those executed properly.

The angle of bank will become reasonably automatic. But, like many pilots, you will probably make the mistake of allowing the airspeed to first decrease then increase as you perform a turn in the landing pattern. You must work at this skill so you keep the nose below the horizon (always below the horizon) at a proper, and constant pitch attitude while performing any turn; but especially turns at low altitude. In this manner, the airspeed will remain constant.

A properly executed turn in the landing pattern takes 5 to 7 seconds. During this brief time you should concentrate on keeping the airspeed constant and the YAW STRING ABSOLUTELY STRAIGHT!

If you keep the nose of the glider below the horizon, use a proper bank angle, keep a constant, correct airspeed, and a straight yaw string, it is virtually impossible to stall. This may be the most important paragraph in this book. Read it again.

As soon as the turn onto base leg is finished, look at the intended touch down point and judge if you are below the steepest possible (5:1) glide slope. Use whatever dive brakes are necessary to keep within the landing cone, and make adjustments from the normal pattern if you are low or high.

Perform another well-banked, constant speed, straight yaw string turn onto the final leg. Try to time the turn so you are aligned with the centerline of the runway as you finish the turn. If you are not aligned with the center of the runway or landing area, make an adjustment as early as possible so you do not need to make additional alignment turns close to the ground.

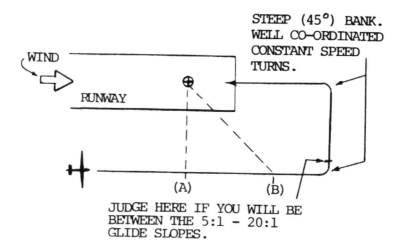

FINAL APPROACH

On final approach, maintain a constant airspeed with the elevator, and control the glide path of the glider to the touch down point with the dive brakes. During this time, the dive brakes are serving as the glide path control.

It is important to maintain a constant pitch attitude so the airspeed remains constant. If the glider becomes too high, open the dive brakes more, increasing drag. Do not allow yourself to push the stick forward in an attempt to make the glider come down quicker. This will not work.

To make the glider come down quicker, you must decrease the glider's performance by opening the dive brakes. Putting the nose down, which increases the airspeed can actually make the glider go further!

If the glider is low in the landing cone, close the dive brakes. Do not pull back on the control stick in a futile attempt to keep the glider up. This will not work.

Slowing down will keep the glider from traveling as far. The only way you can extend the glide is to decrease drag, by closing the dive brakes.

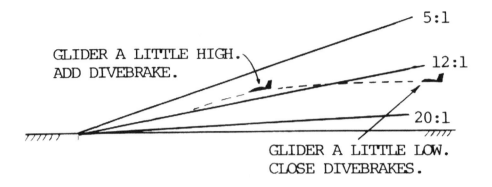

GLIDER A LITTLE HIGH.
ADD DIVEBRAKE.

5:1

12:1

20:1

GLIDER A LITTLE LOW.
CLOSE DIVEBRAKES.

During the final approach, avoid large movements of the dive brakes. As early as possible, try to set the dive brakes to allow an approach with no further adjustment of the dive brakes. Of course, you will usually need some adjustments, but try to recognize the need for an adjustment as early as possible to avoid gross dive brake adjustments.

POINTS THAT MOVE AND DON'T MOVE

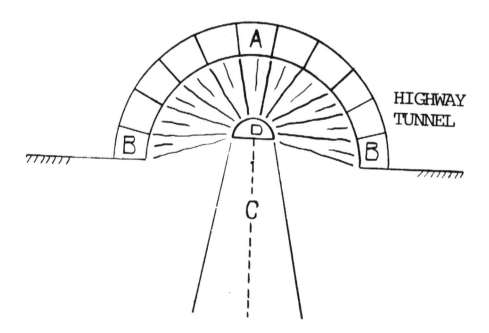

HIGHWAY
TUNNEL

This is a tunnel. As you drive a car towards the tunnel, point "A" will appear to move up the windshield and over the roof. Points "B" will appear to move out the sides of the windshield and around the car, and point "C" will appear to move down the windshield and under the car. Point "D", where the car is going, will appear to remain stationary.

You see a similar effect from snowflakes when driving in a snowstorm. Dead ahead, where you and the car are going, the flakes appear stationary.

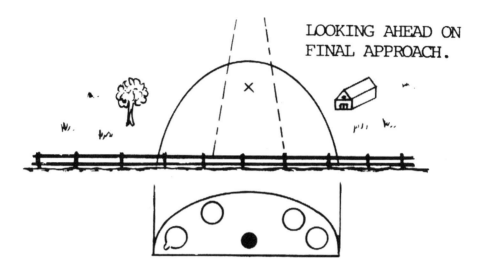

LOOKING AHEAD ON FINAL APPROACH.

This is a view on final approach through the windshield of a glider. If you fly a constant speed, and on the proper glide slope, the tree and the building will appear to move out the sides of the windshield. The fence will move down the windshield, and X, where the glider is going, will remain stationary.

If the X moves down the windshield like the fence, the glider will over-fly the X and will land long, so you need more dive brakes. If the X moves up the windshield like the letter A on the tunnel, you will land short, so you should use less dive brake.

Your natural instincts may incorrectly cause you to "freeze" the touch down point on the windshield by changing the glider pitch attitude with the elevator. But this change in pitch attitude will cause an airspeed change too. Watch the pitch attitude and airspeed closely. Keep them constant.

During your first attempts at landing, it may be easier to see points that move, such as the fence, than it is to see points that don't move.

Your instructor will be watching the airspeed very closely as you fly the landing pattern. It is almost always true if, during the landing, a pilot is incorrectly flying too fast, it is because the glider is too high and the pilot is trying to make the glider come down quicker by incorrectly pushing forward on the control stick. If the airspeed is too slow, the glider is probably too low and the pilot is trying to hold the glider up by incorrectly pulling back on the stick.

Learn to keep the airspeed constant (by keeping a constant pitch attitude with the elevator) and controlling where the glider will touch down (the glide slope) with correct use of the dive brakes or spoilers.

Landings take some practice because so many things are happening at once, and the control sensitivity is constantly changing. As the airspeed dissipates, the controls become less and less responsive.

THE ROUND OUT OR FLARE

If you fly down the glide slope with the dive brakes fully opened, the approach will be steep and the round out will be abrupt.

STEEP APPROACH

This abrupt round out will be difficult to time properly. If you are a bit late, you will hit the ground hard. If you flare too early, you stand the risk of ballooning high into the air again, causing a possible hard landing.

A shallower approach will be easier to accomplish simply because the flare is gentle, and occurs over a longer period of time.

SHALLOW APPROACH

It is important to maintain a constant approach speed all the way to the flare point.

The exact height the flare is begun is not critical. Usually, you begin the flare with a small backward movement of the stick about 20 - 30 feet high so the glider is flown level about 2 - 5 feet above the ground.

As you begin the flare, it is important to lift your eyes and look well ahead. In this way you will be better able to judge the height of the glider above the ground with your peripheral vision.

At the end of the flare, you should be just inches above the ground. The dive brakes end their duty as the glide path control, and now become the "touch down control."

If you have misjudged the approach and are landing short of the intended point, you can allow the glider to "float" just above the ground for a considerable distance simply by closing the dive brakes. This provides a very precise method of touching down on a particular spot.

The idea is to keep the glider just above the ground while the airspeed dissipates by gently applying more and more back stick pressure, without rising above the ground any higher. Eventually, the glider cannot be kept airborne and it touches down with the main wheel and tail wheel (or tail skid) touching the ground simultaneously.

After touch down, the dive brake handle becomes the "stopping control." On many training gliders, the dive brake handle is connected to the wheel brake. Deploying the dive brakes fully actuates the wheel brake. You can roll along the ground for some distance before stopping the glider.

The dive brakes have three distinct functions:

1. Glide path control.
2. Touch down control.
3. Stopping control (on many gliders).

THE TOUCH DOWN

When you eventually fly cross country, you will learn touching down at a very slow airspeed is important because the slowest speed at touch down gives the shortest possible ground roll after landing. A short roll out may prevent unnecessary damage to the glider from stones or holes in a field. For this reason, you should practice slow speed landings most of the time. Higher touch down airspeeds should be used in turbulent or cross wind conditions.

Landing at the slowest possible speed, you might touch down with the tail wheel first. This is not undesirable on an off field landing, but may put unnecessary stress on the glider during day-to-day use.

After the flare, you should hold the glider very close to the ground and allow the glider to slow down, and then touch down in a tail-low attitude. The nose wheel or skid, if so equipped, should never be permitted to touch the ground first because of stress and wear.

It is important for you to realize you do not *make* the glider land. The glider should touch down when it can no longer stay airborne. Do not force the glider to land prematurely, or at high speeds.

Touching down on the wheel at a slow airspeed is excellent preparation for your eventual cross country training and flights.

THE ROLL OUT

After the glider touches down, it is important not to relax. The flight hasn't ended. The flight ends only when the glider comes to a complete stop.

After touchdown, keep the wings level (upwind wing low if there is a crosswind) and steer the glider with the rudder. You may tend to want to bank the wings to turn the glider as you would in the air. But while the glider is on the ground, you steer with the rudder and keep the wings level. Tilting the wings too much can cause a wing tip to touch the ground, which can cause the glider to swerve violently (ground loop).

Never roll the glider near other gliders, people or other objects. Your judgment will not be very accurate until you have made hundreds of landings. Experienced, skillful pilots never take unnecessary risks.

After touchdown, gently and gradually continue with the backward stick motion to keep the tail down, reducing the loads on the front wheel or skid if the glider is so equipped.

BALLOONING

A brisk backwards pull on the stick as you are beginning the flare, might cause the glider to "balloon" back into the air just as you are about to land. A balloon will also occur if the glider lands hard and bounces back into the air. Pilots instinctively move the stick forward at the first sign of the glider ballooning. This can result in a hard landing and another, worse balloon. If a balloon occurs you should do one of the following:

If the balloon is only a few feet into the air, hold the controls so the glider is level with the ground and allow it to settle back onto the ground. You probably need to close the dive brakes as the glider begins to balloon, and then re-open them as you perform a second flare.

If the balloon is five feet or more into the air, close the dive brakes if open, be sure to ease the stick forward, get the nose back down into a normal gliding attitude so the glider does not stall, then make another attempt at the flare and touch down. Try very hard not to over-control the glider.

NO NO'S IN THE LANDING PATTERN

It is almost never correct to perform a 360-degree turn below 1,000 feet AGL (Above Ground Level) in the landing pattern. You might be tempted to do this if you find yourself too high somewhere in the pattern. You may even get away with it, which will encourage you to do it again. Sooner or later you will lose more altitude than you expect, and end up low, perhaps causing an accident. No 360's in the pattern!

Another serious hazard is low altitude turns onto the base or final legs. These are caused by losing altitude too quickly during the downwind leg, entering the pattern at a too low an altitude, or excessive use of the dive brakes.

Low altitude turns are hazardous because of low-level turbulence, shear, wind gradient, and psychological problems, which may cause the glider to stall and crash. The pilot must recognize any excess loss of altitude and turn onto the base leg early at a safe altitude even though it means landing further along the runway.

WRITTEN TEST #7 - LANDINGS

1. What is the dive brake open glide ratio of most sailplanes?

2. What is the maximum glide ratio of the trainer you fly?

3. Below 1,000 feet AGL a pilot should never _____?

4. What is the three item pre-landing checklist performed at the I.P.?

5. What is the primary judgmental decision to be made during the downwind leg?

6. What two checkpoints are used during the downwind leg?

7. What is the normal, desired sink rate during the downwind leg?

8. What should you do if you experienced excessive sink during the downwind leg?

9. What would you do if you encountered lift during the downwind leg?

10. How should the turn into base leg be made?

11. Upon completion of the turn onto base leg, you realize that you are too high. What will you do?

12. You are on base leg ready to turn into final and realize you are too high. There is one type of pattern that should be avoided. What is it?

13. On final it is important to maintain a constant _____ using the _____ control, and "freeze" the desired touchdown point on the windshield using which control?

14. On final you realize that you are above the 5:1 glide slope. As a student pilot you should _____?

15. As an experienced pilot, when might you find the TLAR method most useful?

Answers on page 153

Schempp-Hirth Discus
Courtesy Schempp-Hirth Sailplanes

Premature Termination Of The Tow

During the aero tow, there is one possible emergency to consider. It can be classified under the heading of "premature termination of the tow". This could include such emergencies as engine failure, tow plane running out of gas, or most common, rope breaks. It is important to realize these occasions DO arise even if they happen infrequently! There's really no excuse for not being prepared for this emergency. Before take off, mentally prepare yourself for a rope break and have a plan of action. Your mind, and left hand, should be ready to pull the release.

A premature termination of a tow is anything that causes the aero tow to cease before the pilot intended. A rope break or other event that occurs above 600 feet usually causes no one any serious concern, but the same occurrence at low altitude has resulted in many accidents. This chapter discusses some of the possibilities and suggests procedures a pilot can use in case an emergency occurs.

A premature termination of a tow can occur in a variety of ways.

1. Rope break.

2. Engine failure of the tow plane (partial or total).

3. Release mechanism failure (tow plane or glider).

4. Accidental release (passenger or pilot of glider or tow plane).

5. Fire or smoke in tow plane (real or imaginary).

6. Bird strike, bee sting, or other critter problem.

7. Ground loop.

8. People and/or pets running out onto the runway.

9. Discovery of forgotten preflight item, such as failure to hook up controls.

10. Others I haven't thought of.

"Anything can happen ON THIS TOW" should be the last thought a glider pilot, or the tow pilot, should have as the tow begins.

After your early training flights, aero-tow becomes easier and the actual flying of the aircraft becomes more or less automatic. At this point, well before solo, at the beginning of each aero-tow, a great deal of your concentration should be given to what you will do when the rope breaks on tow.

The most critical period is during the first 600 feet of altitude or so. After you have gained 600 feet, there is more time to react to an emergency and you will have more options.

Pilots who have been trained on a winch launch are better prepared for rope breaks. During a typical winch training course a student pilot will experience several cable breaks (real and simulated), and witness even more by other pilots. Things occur rapidly on a winch tow, and often when the glider is in an extreme nose high attitude. The glider pilot must be prepared to react instantly and correctly. Every winch pilot has a specific plan of action should the cable break at any time. So should the pilots who launch by aero tow.

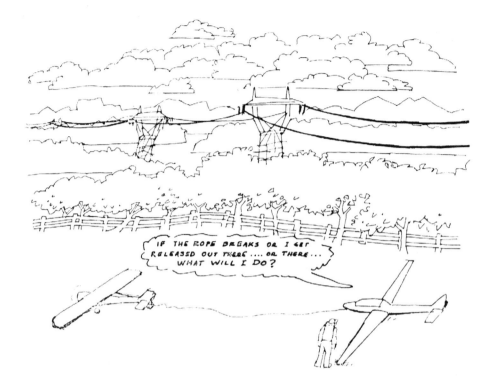

We should inspect the winch pilot's training and incorporate what we can into our own plan of action should our tow rope fail.

The winch pilot is *ready*. The left hand is on the release knob at the beginning of the tow and remains there until release.

I don't know any instructor who teaches students to have their hand on the release knob during an aero-tow. (Maybe we are afraid the student will release inadvertently). You should at least have your left hand very near the release during the early stages of the aero-tow. (Having your hand on the release knob during a tow in heavy turbulence is probably not a good idea.)

Many of the top competition pilots have their hand on the release knob at the beginning of the tow, just in case they lose control at an early stage of the launch.

Very frequently, the rope breaks during the first part of tow, well before the sailplane is airborne. This is when the strain on the rope is the greatest, not withstanding any jerks as the slack comes out during the tow.

The reason the rope breaks at this early stage is because it is worn out, frayed, cut or perhaps because a knot has formed. A knot can reduce the strength of a rope by nearly 50%. It isn't practical to inspect every inch of the tow rope before each and every tow, but the glider pilot should inspect the rope near the tow ring where it is under the greatest strain and also watch the rope for knots as the tow plane pulls the slack out. Remember, the responsibility for preflighting the tow rope lies with the pilot in command of the glider.

120

If the rope should break at a very early stage, there isn't much to be concerned about. Simply roll to a stop. But if you are moving along at 10 m.p.h. or perhaps just about to become airborne, you will have to keep calm and avoid running into anything or anyone. It's surprising how difficult it is to find the wheel brake under a high stress situation when you are not prepared.

If you are airborne when the rope breaks, you may have to act quickly to prevent overrunning the end of the runway. The first step on any rope break while airborne will be to lower the nose to maintain flying speed. A stall from even five feet of altitude can cause significant damage. The second step is to get your hand on the dive brake handle in order to control where you will touch down and stop.

At this point we are assuming you are able to land and stop straight ahead on the runway. Now let's backtrack and suppose you didn't have a rope break. Let's suppose instead that it was a partial or catastrophic engine failure in the tow plane. This puts a whole new light on the problem because now you must avoid colliding with the tow plane which will be landing on the same runway, and is connected by a tow rope only 200 feet in front of you!

Under these circumstances the tow plane is *supposed* to release the tow rope and land on the left side of the runway and taxi off the left edge to avoid a collision, and the glider is *supposed* to release the tow rope and land on the right side of the runway and taxi off the right edge of the runway. (Notice both of the aircraft are turning the same as they would from a normal release from tow.)

Suppose instead of an engine failure the tow pilot had a fire onboard. As you can imagine, there isn't anything more terrifying for a power pilot than fire. Your tow pilot may panic. You might not be able to see the fire from the glider. What you will see happen is a sudden loss of power and the tow plane descending back to the runway. The tow pilot may even jump out of the tow plane before it comes to a complete stop. Perhaps the engine is still running and the tow plane might ground loop and start coming towards your glider with that big propeller turning.

In these last two scenarios you can see the importance of the glider pilot being able to react quickly to the situation. In both cases the tow plane pilot is under high stress and may not pull the release. (In many cases the tow plane release knob is in a dumb place.) The glider pilot must be prepared to release instantly in order to avoid a collision. (Tow pilots should be briefed for this emergency so they turn the engine off.)

> The rule during the first few hundred feet of aero-tow should be that you, the glider pilot, have your hand near the release knob ready to act in an emergency.

YOUR LEFT HAND

There are three likely plans of action for your left hand:

1. Pull the release knob in case of a tow emergency.
2. Push the dive brakes closed in case you fail to lock them before takeoff.
3. Grab the canopy in case you fail to lock it before takeoff.

If you have your left hand on the release knob, just rest your fingertips on it to avoid an accidental release.

Now on to the next phase. You find yourself too high to land and stop straight ahead on the runway, but too low to do a 180-degree turn back to the runway. In this case you will have to land somewhere else. Where you go should have been determined before you took off.

One of the serious mistakes pilots make before they fly at a new site is failing to ask the local pilots what they would do if a rope break should occur. There are a number of possible ways to handle this emergency. You might be able to land on a different runway (turns up to 90 degrees may be possible, but be careful not to try this too low!) More likely, you will have to land in one of the available farmer's fields beyond the end of the runway. Maybe there is no place to make a safe landing and you will have to crash into trees, land in a lake, or whatever. The important point is to ask for advice from local pilots before flying at a strange site.

In case of a rope break:

1. Be sure to lower the nose of the glider to maintain flying speed.

2. Release remaining tow rope only if you have time. (This is usually not extremely important.)

3. You may turn either right or left. This is an emergency and not a normal tow release.

4. Minor turns can be made regardless of altitude. In general, below 200 feet your limit should be no more than 90 degrees in direction (not bank angle.) But don't continue a turn so long you catch a wing tip on the ground.

The most serious mistake that can be made is to attempt to do a 180-degree turn back to the runway at an insufficient altitude.

If you are too low to complete the 180-degree turn, you will most likely stall and spin or strike the ground with a wing tip causing the glider to cartwheel. In either case it is almost impossible to avoid serious injuries.

Normally, the minimum altitude from which a glider pilot can safely accomplish a 180-degree turn is 200 feet. This minimum altitude would have to be raised to take into consideration aircraft performance, pilot abilities, wind, and density altitude. For instance, 200 feet is quite safe for a Schweizer 2-33 near sea level but a heavy, slow-rolling sailplane in the high mountains might not be able to do a safe 180-degree turn below 300 or 400 feet.

Remember, everyone's instinctive reaction is to attempt the 180-degree turn and return to the field. It takes a strong, disciplined, well-trained pilot to react properly to this emergency. No matter how much you read, no matter how much you are told, you are not likely to react properly unless you fully understand the problem, have a plan of action, overcome your instinctive reactions and do the pre-planned best thing.

It is far better to spend a few hours retrieving a sailplane from a farmer's field than to take months getting a sailplane repaired. Don't take any unnecessary chances. Even if you are above 200 feet, it still might be better to land in that giant farm field that requires no risk than to attempt a low turn you have never practiced.

The magic 200 foot minimum height is nearly universally accepted by textbooks and instructors around the world. If you experimented by first trying a 180-degree turn at 200 feet and then lowering this minimum turn-around altitude on subsequent test flights you would find that a 180-degree turn can be made at lower altitudes in these test conditions. The 200 foot minimum altitude takes into consideration the element of total surprise, the subsequent slow reaction time, and perhaps not totally perfect flying finesse of a pilot who is not as sharp as we sometimes misguide ourselves into believing we are. The firm rule is, NEVER ATTEMPT A 180-degree RE-TURN TO THE FIELD BELOW 200 FEET. And, decide before you take off if conditions call for a higher limit.

How do you know you are above 200 feet? The only reliable way is to monitor the altimeter during this stage of the aero-tow. The altimeter has an unavoidable lag error, but this error benefits the glider pilot in that the glider will be higher than the altimeter shows.

Get into the habit of making note of the critical altimeter reading before each takeoff. Say to yourself, "OK, my altimeter is set at the field elevation of 1,250 feet. That means my critical altitude in case of a rope break is 1,450 feet." You now know what your responses will be. Below 1,450 feet you will land straight ahead. Above 1,450 feet you know you can turn around because you are more than 200 feet above the ground.

Here's an important habit to get into: AS YOU PASS THROUGH 200 FEET, OR YOUR PREDETERMINED DECISION ALTITUDE, ANNOUNCE IT OUT LOUD: "200 FEET."

If the rope breaks and you haven't announced 200 feet out loud, you know what your response will be. Land ahead! If you have announced 200 feet out loud, you know you can perform a safe 180-degree turn. No student is permitted to solo at our school unless the student reliably announces aloud "200 feet" on every flight. Any solo student, who fails to announce the 200-foot mark on subsequent training flights or check rides, automatically receives a simulated rope break. Every student, including transition pilots, receives at least three rope break simulations before solo; one straight ahead rope break at the maximum altitude that still permits a straight ahead landing on the runway, and two 200 foot rope breaks.

Being able to make a safe 180-degree turn back to the field from 200 feet doesn't always mean you should. If you are above 200 feet and the rope breaks, your decision whether to turn back to the field or not is based on several factors:

1. Pilot currency. How sharp are your piloting skills?

2. Available emergency fields. Is a big, no-risk field ahead of you?

3. Distance from the airport. Perhaps you are at 200 feet but too far from the airport to make it back. A hot, humid day would cause the tow plane not to climb as rapidly as a cooler day.

4. Wind. Perhaps the subsequent tailwind is too strong for a safe downwind landing.

5. Tow plane performance. Sometimes you gain so much altitude so fast that you might not be able to land and stop on the runway if you did turn around. (Especially when taking off into a strong wind.)

THE 180-DEGREE TURN

Refer to the following chart. Notice the minimum altitude loss vs. angle of bank shows the optimum angle of bank is 45 degrees. You lose less altitude performing a 45 degree banked turn.

There are other reasons to use a well-banked turn. Without going into detail, the prime cause of the stall and spin during any turn close to the ground is the over use of the rudder in a subconscious attempt to make the aircraft turn quicker, coupled with the incorrect, but instinctive attempt to hold the aircraft up with back stick pressure.

Angle of bank	Speed, knots	Sink Rate knots	Load factor	Radius of turn feet	Time for 360°, second	Altitude lost in 360°, ft.
60	64	3.92	2.0	208	12.1	80
50	56	2.69	1.6	236	15.6	71
45	54	2.34	1.4	255	17.7	70
40	52	2.07	1.3	281	20.3	71
35	50	1.87	1.2	315	23.5	74
30	48	1.72	1.2	361	27.7	81
25	47	1.61	1.1	427	33.5	91
20	47	1.52	1.1	528	42.2	108
15	46	1.46	1.0	698	56.5	140
10	46	1.42	1.0	1040	85.0	204
0	45	1.39	1.0	–	–	–

Circling performance of the Standard Libelle at an all-up weight of 695 lbs. near sea-level.

The best and safest turn close to the ground, (but more than a half wing span above the ground and without a wind gradient or turbulence) is a 45 degree angle of bank. Regardless of the angle of bank you use, you must maintain a safe speed and keep the yaw string straight. Your glider cannot stall or spin if you obey this rule.

If the rope breaks, your decision as to what to do should be automatic. If you have announced "200 feet" you may turn around. If you have decided to perform a 180-degree turn, you must primarily pay attention to the airspeed and the yaw string. (Angle of bank becomes automatic with practice.)

WHICH WAY TO TURN

If you have decided to turn back to the runway, you should normally first turn into the wind. The wind will help keep you lined up with the runway and give you a shorter ground distance to travel. However, you may also have additional considerations to avoid obstructions by turning away from hills, trees, buildings, etc. Before takeoff, think about which way you'll turn if the rope breaks.

AIRSPEED

The airspeed you use cannot be too slow, (you might stall), nor too fast. (You can't waste precious altitude with excessive speed.) The speed to use during this 180-degree turn should be the normal pattern airspeed, plus an arbitrary 5 miles per hour because it is an emergency. (Sometimes called the "wife and kids factor".)

Once the turn is accomplished, you will usually have a tailwind. You must maintain flying speed. Your *ground speed* will be much faster than normal, therefore giving an illusion of a faster *airspeed*, possibly causing a stall. Glance at the airspeed indicator more frequently than during a normal, into-the-wind landing.

124

Drop the remaining tow rope only if it is convenient. Land, and then stop in a big open area. Remember the last 100 feet or so of the landing roll with a tailwind may be without directional control. Never attempt to taxi into a crowded area when landing downwind.

In summation, there are several key points to watch for during every flight and especially during simulated rope breaks:

1. Just before take-off, are you thinking what you will do in case the rope breaks? Which way will you turn? Is 200 feet the correct minimum altitude for a 180-degree turn on this flight?

2. During the aero-tow are your fingertips on or near the release knob?

3. Do you always announce 200 feet out loud? (Or a higher altitude, if appropriate.)

4. On simulated rope breaks, do you first lower the nose of the glider to maintain airspeed?

5. During any turn close to the ground, do you maintain a steady, correct airspeed, and keep your yaw string absolutely straight?

One last point is the path the tow plane follows on take-off. The normal way is to fly along the center line of the runway. In case of a rope break the glider pilot will need to make an additional turn at low level to get aligned with the runway, which can be very dangerous . . .

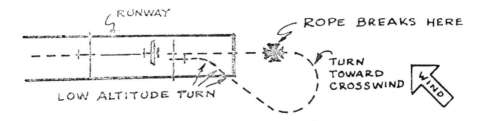

If the tow pilot would simply drift slightly downwind during the first 200 - 400 feet of climb, it would make a rope break safer for the glider pilot by eliminating that additional turn.

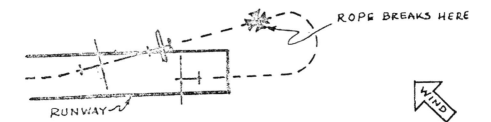

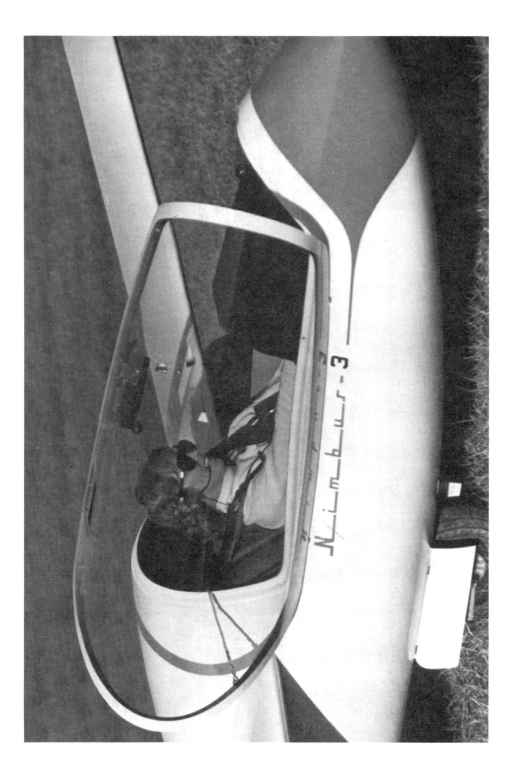

SLIPS

A slip is a descent with one wing lowered and the glider's longitudinal axis aligned at an angle to the flight path. A slip might be used for two purposes: to create extra drag to steepen the descent rate without increasing airspeed, and to enable the aircraft to fly a straight ground track while landing in a crosswind by "side slipping" through the air enough to counteract the drift caused by the wind.

At one time, glider's did not have glide path control devices such as spoilers, dive brakes, and flaps. Pilots used the slip to create additional drag to control where they would touch down. Slips are now used primarily for landings in crosswinds and for clearing tall obstructions on off-field landings. Every so often, a pilot might misjudge the landing approach so severely they must resort to the side slip in addition to the dive brakes.

The use of slips has limitations. Some pilots may develop the habit to lose altitude with violent slipping rather than with a smooth application of the controls and exercising good judgment so only a slight or moderate slip is required. In a real emergency, this kind of erratic behavior will eventually lead to trouble, because the excessive speed can easily result in preventing a touchdown anywhere near the intended touchdown point.

A forward slip is a slip in which the glider's direction continues along the same ground path as before the slip. This would be typically used to lose altitude while flying on final approach with the glider on the proper ground track but too high. If there is a crosswind, the slip will be much more effective if made toward the side from which the wind is blowing. Always slip into the wind.

Beginning with the glider in straight glide, the wing on the side toward which the slip is to be made should be lowered by using the ailerons. At the same time, the aircraft's nose must be yawed in the opposite direction by applying opposite rudder. This results in the aircraft's longitudinal axis being at an angle to its original flight path. The amount the nose is yawed in the opposite direction from the bank should be such that the original ground track is maintained. Airspeed must be kept steady by maintaining the same pitch attitude and not allowing the nose to pitch down.

Because of the location of the pitot tube and static vents, the airspeed indication may have considerable error when the glider is in a slip. You must be aware of this and recognize a properly performed slip by the attitude of the glider, the sound of the airflow, and the feel of the controls.

To discontinue the slip, level the wings with the ailerons, and simultaneously release the rudder pressure, while adjusting the stick pressure to maintain a constant airspeed. If you release the rudder pressure too abruptly, the nose will swing too quickly into line or may yaw in the other direction and the glider will tend to gain excess speed.

If you are using a slip during the last portions of the landing, be careful to align the fuselage of the glider with the runway prior to touchdown so the glider is pointed in the same direction it is traveling over the ground. This requires the pilot to use timely action to discontinue the slip at just the right moment. Failure to do so may result in severe side loads on the undercarriage. It may also result in a violent groundloop or the glider turning uncontrollably toward the side of the runway.

A sideslip is distinguished from a forward slip only in the fact that in a sideslip the longitudinal axis of the aircraft remains parallel to the original flight path, but the flight path "slips" sideways according to the steepness of the bank. The sideslip is important in counter-acting wind drift during crosswind landings.

You may be concerned about the glider being flown in a cross-controlled manner during a slip. Since the airspeed indicator often is erratic and may even read 0 airspeed during an extreme slip, you may naturally assume this is a dangerous flight attitude. As you have found out by now, crossed control stalls can be very dangerous.

In a crossed-control stall, the aircraft will always drop the wing that has the highest angle of attack, which means the wing with the down aileron. In a slip, the aircraft has the down aileron on the high wing, so the high wing would tend to stall first. This is possible, but it also means a stall would take a long time to develop, and you would surely recognize the problem and take action.

In addition to the time delay, to recover from a crossed control stall, you would apply opposite rudder to the rotation. In a slip, you are holding rudder pressure opposite to the bank angle, so the glider would again have to go "over the top" and rotate in the opposite direction to the slip if it did stall. For your own understanding, you should try stalling the glider from slips so you are aware of how it reacts. Have your instructor demonstrate this, then try it. Your instructor will keep you out of trouble and correct any flying errors.

There is a particular hazard you should be aware of: Suppose you are on base leg of the landing pattern as depicted in the next drawing. The wind is blowing across the runway in the direction indicated. You decide you are too high and need to slip. You may be tempted to enter the slip as you turn onto final. This is very dangerous because you're turning left while holding the controls crossed: you're holding rudder in the direction of the turn (the dreaded skidding turn), and opposite aileron. While turning, entering a sideslip opposite to the direction of the turn can lead to a stall-spin because you are holding the controls as necessary to enter the spin. Wait until you are lined up on final approach before you initiate the slip with the wing down on the "outside" of the turn.

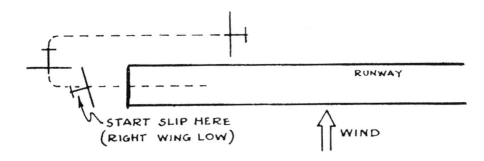

If the wind were blowing from the opposite direction in our example, you would be able to safely enter a slip during the turn onto final because you would be holding the controls in a recover-from-a-turning-stall manner.

CAUTION: As a rule of thumb, simply avoid entering a slip while in a turn.

You can practice slips at altitude by trying to fly along a road, or fence row while performing a side slip. Try to have a smooth entry, and a smooth recovery, while maintaining a steady airspeed. You should be able to side slip in both directions equally well.

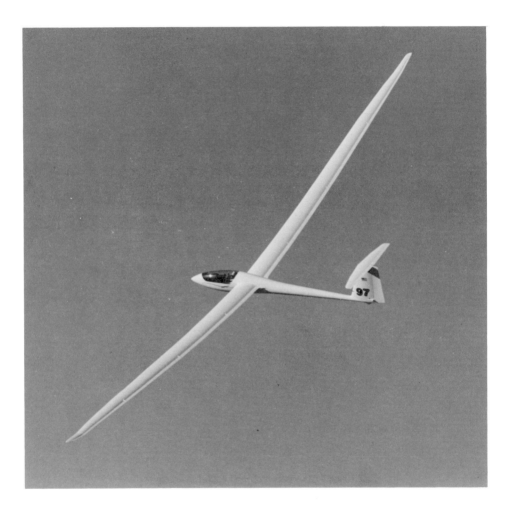

CROSSWIND LANDING

You sometimes must land with the wind blowing across the runway. The same basic principles apply to the crosswind landing as a normal landing. Only the additional techniques required for correcting for wind drift need to be discussed. (See also the chapter on slips).

Crosswind landings are more difficult than crosswind takeoffs because it is more difficult to maintain control while the airspeed is decreasing rather than increasing speed as on takeoff.

There are two methods of handling the crosswind approach and landings: the crab method and the wing-low or slip method. The crab method is the easiest method during the approach phase of the landing, but requires a high degree of judgment and timing to remove the crab immediately before touchdown. The wing-low, side slip method is recommended in most situations, but you may find it is often desirable to use a combination of the two methods.

The crab method is established by assuming a heading into the wind with the wings level so the glider's ground track remains aligned with the centerline of the runway. Note the yaw string would remain streamlined. The crab angle would be held until just prior to touchdown, when the glider must be quickly aligned with the runway, using the rudder, to avoid any sideward contact with the runway.

Allowing the glider to touch down before the crab angle is removed can cause the glider to ground loop, or otherwise lose control. A pilot may also use the crab method until just before round out and then smoothly change over to the wing-low method for the touchdown. (Changing technique during the round out phase requires more pilot skill).

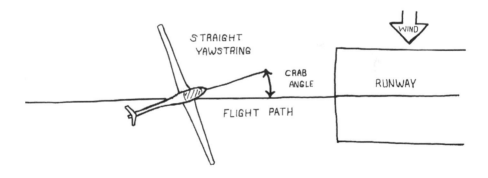

The wing-low method also compensates for wind drift, but in addition, enables the pilot to maintain the longitudinal axis of the glider in line with the ground track and centerline of the runway throughout the final leg, round out, flare, and touchdown. This prevents the possibility of touching down sideways, which can cause a dangerous ground loop or produce damaging side loads on the landing gear.

To use the wing-low method, simply align the glider's heading with the centerline of the runway, note the direction and amount of drift, then apply drift correction by side slipping into the wind by lowering the upwind wing. The amount the wing needs to be lowered depends on the strength of the wind.

When the wing is lowered, the glider will tend to turn in that direction. It is necessary to simultaneously apply sufficient opposite rudder to prevent the turn and keep the glider's longitudinal axis aligned with the runway. The drift is being controlled with bank angle, and the heading with the rudder. The glider is now side slipping just enough to offset the drift created by the crosswind.

If the glider begins to move off the centerline of the runway, it is an easy matter to either increase the bank angle, or decrease the rudder to re-align things.

In a very strong crosswind, the glider's rudder may not be powerful enough to permit a severe slip. In this case a combination of the wing-low and crab methods will be necessary.

Your glider has a maximum crosswind landing capability. Generally it is not possible to control the landing rollout in direct crosswinds of more than 15 knots. If there is a strong crosswind you should use a different runway, or possibly, if the landing area is large enough, land diagonally across the runway, thus lessening the crosswind component.

CROSSWIND ROUND OUT (FLARE)

Generally, the round out will be made as in a normal landing. But you will have to continue holding crosswind correction to prevent drifting. As the airspeed decreases, the flight controls become less effective, so you may have to gradually increase the deflection of the rudder and ailerons to maintain the proper drift correction.

CROSSWIND TOUCHDOWN

At the point of touchdown, do not level the wings. Keep the upwind wing low throughout the flare and touchdown. If you level the wings, the glider will begin to drift, causing side loads on the undercarriage and a possible ground loop.

CAUTION: It is possible to touch the upwind wing on the ground and cause a severe ground loop. If you are flying a low-wing glider or are flying in a strong crosswind, be careful not to have the wing so low it touches the ground!

If you have been using the crab method of drift correction, the crab will have to be removed with the rudder before touchdown to prevent side loads on the undercarriage. This requires precise timing and judgment.

If you have been using the wing-low method, the wing should remain low throughout the flare and touchdown. Gliders have a particular advantage over power planes in this respect, because the pilot of a power plane is unable to keep the wings tilted until the plane stops. The power plane will eventually settle on all three wheels despite the efforts of the pilot.

After touchdown, be very alert to any tendency for the glider to swing out of control. Don't relax, and don't attempt to taxi near other aircraft or people. During the last few yards of the roll out, you will have very little control of the glider. As the glider's rudder loses effectiveness, the glider will tend to weathervane into the wind. You should keep the upwind wing low during the roll out, and ideally, the upwind wing should come to rest on the ground as the glider stops.

If it is gusty, or the winds are strong, it will be very much more difficult to perform a landing in crosswind conditions.

STEEP TURNS

Continuous steep turns are often the most difficult maneuver for pilots to perform during the FAA flight test. Power pilots who are transitioning into gliders find this maneuver particularly difficult. The reason is because it is seldom a power pilot would make a continuous turn. In fact, most turns in a power plane are seldom more than 180 degrees.

Turns are supposed to be precise. Coordination should be perfect, and airspeed control should be accurate. The most common faults are incorrect use of the rudder during the entry into the turn, slipping or skidding during the turn, using excessive speed (or the inability to maintain a steady speed), and not being able to recover on a specific heading.

To practice steep turns (40-45 degree angle of bank or more), you should begin by practicing coordinated entry into, and out of, shallow turns. Perform several roll-ins and roll-outs of a turn. Are you able to keep the yaw string centered? The more quickly you move the ailerons, the more difficult the coordination with the rudder. Start by gently rolling into the turn and gradually build up to a more brisk turn entry into a steeper bank angle.

As an aircraft is banked into a turn, the nose wants to lower on the horizon. This happens because the aircraft is heavier during a turn due to centrifugal force. Since the CG is forward of the center of pressure, there is now required more down load on the tail surfaces to maintain a constant airspeed. If you don't resist it, the airspeed will naturally want to increase.

To avoid this happening, before you roll into the turn, note the pitch attitude with the horizon. As you roll into the turn, pay particular attention to the position of the nose in relation to the horizon. Notice the nose does not begin to show signs of lowering until well into the turn (about 30 degrees of arc). Maintain the same pitch attitude by increasing the back pressure on the control stick as needed while the bank angle increases. With practice you should be able to maintain a constant airspeed as you roll into a steeply banked turn, and at the same time maintain a straight yaw string.

While circling, watch the horizon, not the airspeed indicator. By watching the horizon, you will be able to notice any pitch attitude changes which cause the airspeed to change, long before the airspeed actually changes. You will also have the benefit of seeing the yaw string at the same time, so you can adjust for any minor yaw corrections. All of this will make you fly more precisely, and you gain another important benefit.

While you are watching the horizon and the yaw string, you will also be watching outside for other aircraft. This will make you a safer pilot, and at the same time make you a better soaring pilot because you will begin to notice other sailplanes, dust devils, cumulus clouds, etc. for signs of lift. Expert glider pilots spend most of their time looking outside the glider for indications of lift; beginners spend too much time looking inside the glider at the instrument panel.

What speed should you fly during a steep turn? About the only time you do continuous steep turns is while thermalling (or taking flight tests). While thermalling, you will want to fly the best speed for minimum sink at the angle of bank you are using. (More information about speed-to-fly will be found in the training book, "After Solo.") Many factors enter into the formulation of the exact best speed to fly in this circumstance. Fortunately, the performance curve of the glider shows at minimum sinking speeds, the curve is reasonably flat so we have a wide speed range to use without being penalized.

The minimum sinking speed for our particular glider is, perhaps 40 knots. This is the minimum sinking speed for straight gliding flight. In a turn, the minimum sinking speed will increase because centrifugal force causes the glider to weigh more (the wing loading increases). You can simply add another 5 knots to the speed and be reasonably close to the optimum speed for bank angles up to about 30 degrees. Steeper angles of bank will require even higher airspeeds. If you are carrying water ballast, the extra load will require you to add another 5 knots to the airspeed. If the air is turbulent you may need to add a few knots to maintain adequate control. Some sailplanes seem to climb better at what otherwise would be an excessive airspeed.

For steeper angles of bank, the airspeed must either be increased before the bank angle increases, or better, allowed to increase as the bank becomes steeper. As the bank angle is assumed, considerable back pressure must be applied to provide the necessary angle of attack for the increased load.

The outer wing is flying a greater distance than the inner wing during turns, and therefore has a greater airflow over it, which creates greater lift than the inner wing. This unequal amount of lift creates an over-banking tendency which must be overcome to prevent the glider from increasing its bank angle. To counteract this over-banking tendency, you will need to hold steady, opposite aileron pressure during steep turns.

For the flight test you will be expected to select an appropriate airspeed for the bank angle and be able to maintain a steady airspeed during the turns while maintaining coordinated flight. Being able to recover or stop turning on a prescribed heading or towards some object on the horizon is simply a matter of practice. Begin your recovery 10 degrees or so before you come to the desired heading.

GROUND REFERENCE MANEUVERS

The requirements for solo flight include flight training in "ground reference maneuvers." The reason for this requirement is to impress upon the pilot the effect of wind on the ground track of the aircraft as the pilot flies around some ground flight path. In addition to the practical aspects of these maneuvers, the pilot must understand the misleading visual effects caused by the wind while flying at low altitudes.

Flying Straight With No Wind

An aircraft flying straight with the yaw string straight, will fly in a straight line from point to point, in the direction it is pointed.

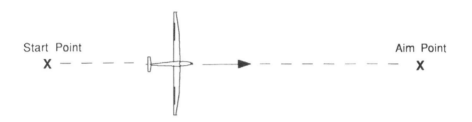

Flying Straight With Wind

If the air mass is moving, (the wind is blowing) the aircraft is affected in one of three ways;

If there is a headwind, the aircraft will have a reduced ground speed.

If there is a tailwind, the aircraft will have an increased ground speed.

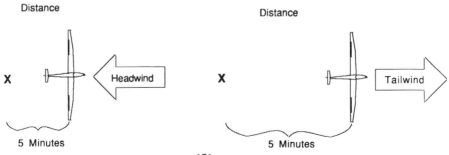

135

Flying at low altitudes with a tailwind creates a potential hazard, because of the illusion of speed. The tailwind causes a false impression of a high speed as the ground rushes by. The pilot may falsely interpret this high ground speed and attempt to slow the aircraft to what looks and feels like the normal speed used on a normal, into the wind, landing. As an example, imagine a glider flying with a 20 knot tailwind. If the glider was flying at 50 knots airspeed, the ground would be rushing by at 70 knots groundspeed. Should the pilot incorrectly attempt to fly the glider at a 50 knot groundspeed, it would require the glider to fly at only 30 knots, which, in most gliders is not possible. It would stall.

When flying at low altitudes with a tailwind, it is very important to frequently check the airspeed indicator. Trim the aircraft for the proper airspeed, and keep the nose of the glider in the normal, below the horizon attitude. Resist any temptation to slow down.

The temptation to slow down will be strongest when flying downwind on a rectangular flight path around a field at low altitude. The downwind leg at the corresponding increased groundspeed, will cause this leg to occur quickly, and the pilot may attempt to slow events down by unconsciously slowing down.

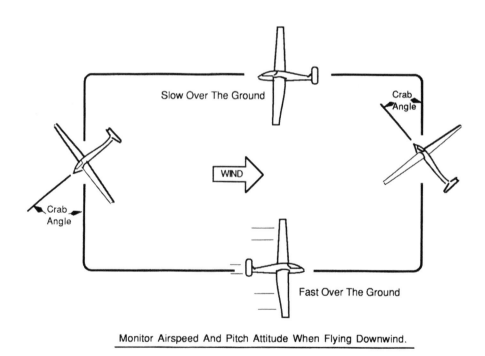

Monitor Airspeed And Pitch Attitude When Flying Downwind.

FLYING IN A CROSSWIND

If the glider is flown in a straight path with a crosswind, the glider will drift sideways with the wind. If the pilot continuously makes corrections in the direction the glider is pointed so the nose of the glider always points toward the intended goal, the glider's ground track would be a curved line.

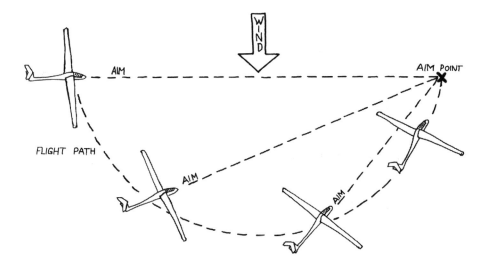

It is more efficient to fly a path through the air to achieve a straight ground track to the goal by pointing the glider into the crosswind. The difference between the ground track and the direction the glider is pointed is called the wind correction angle, or crab angle.

If the crosswind is strong, and the glider is being flown at low altitudes such as in a landing pattern or along a mountain ridge, there will be a strong impression of the glider slipping of skidding through the air, even though the yaw string is centered. The pilot may attempt to fly the glider with a straight ground track by pressing on the rudder to keep the glider pointed in the direction it is traveling.

This is not only inefficient, but the resulting slipping and skidding turns can make the flight hazardous. The pilot must confirm coordination with the yaw string, and fly the glider coordinated at all times.

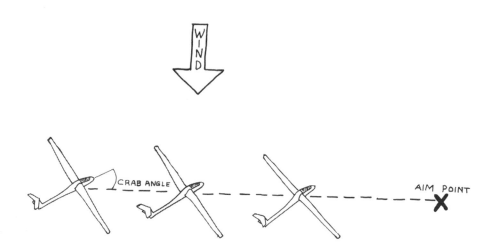

360 Degree Turns With Wind

If the pilot flies a constant bank angle and constant airspeed turn when there is no wind, the flight path over the ground will be the same circular flight path as in the air.

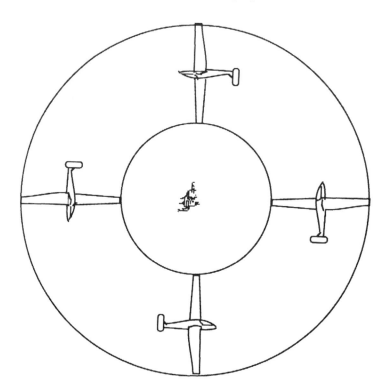

If the pilot flies a constant bank angle and constant airspeed turn when there is a wind, the wind will drift the glider downwind and the result will be a circular flight path through the air. The flight path over the ground, however, will be distorted as shown in the following drawing:

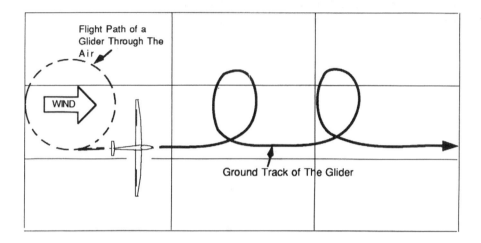

The ground track radius will be greatest when the ground speed is the greatest, which means when the glider is traveling directly downwind. The ground track radius will be the least when the ground speed is least, which is when the glider is flying directly into the wind.

Turns About A Point With Wind

To fly a circular flight path over a point on the ground, the glider pilot will have to vary the angle of bank as the glider turns around the point. When the glider has the greatest groundspeed, the glider must be at it's steepest angle of bank. When the glider has the slowest groundspeed, the glider must be at the shallowest angle of bank.

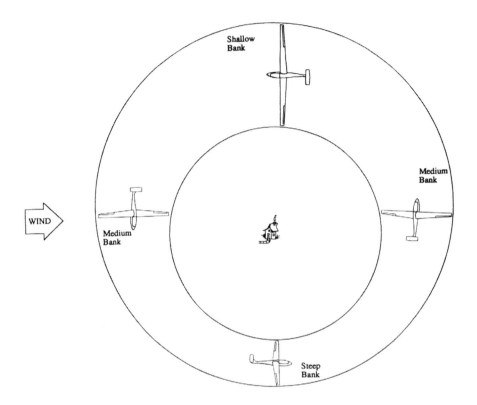

When performing the maneuver, it is best to enter on the downwind leg so the glider will be at it's steepest angle of bank, and at a distance so the bank angle will not be more than 45 degrees. As the maneuver continues, gently reduce the bank angle until the glider is at the shallowest angle on the upwind leg.

After passing the point when the glider is facing directly into the wind, the bank angle would be gently increased until it reaches its maximum bank angle once again on the downwind leg.

While flying the maneuver, it is very important to maintain a constant airspeed, and keep the yaw string centered. Learn to glimpse at the airspeed indicator without staring at it, and control airspeed with a constant pitch attitude.

These maneuvers are generally done at fairly low altitudes. As you descend, be aware of your position relative to the gliderport. Watch out for other aircraft and birds. There may be more turbulence at low altitudes.

SOLO!

If you think you've learned a lot so far, it may interest you to know you will learn far more while you fly solo. Your instructor knows the best time for you to solo. You won't be allowed to go until you have fulfilled all the requirements of the Federal Aviation Regulations, and have shown mastery of the aircraft. One day, after several dual flights the instructor will calmly get out, fasten the rear seat belts, and say, "OK, this time you'll do it yourself."

With a lump in your throat, off you'll go on a flight much like the last several, but one you won't forget for the rest of your life.

Be sure to do a complete pre-takeoff checklist. Are you within the weight and balance limitations for solo flight?

Stay well within the student training area during this and subsequent solo flights.

The instructor may suggest several maneuvers to be done on this flight. You'll be thrilled you really can do this yourself. All too soon the flight will end among handshakes, applause and a cut-off shirttail. Welcome to membership in an exclusive club!

Subsequent training will consist of more dual flights but mostly more and more solo practice and freedom. You will be watched closely for any faults. Your instructor will help you organize your solo flights so you can eventually fulfill the requirements for a private license.

Dual flights will consist of new maneuvers and proficiency check flights. Your instructor will watch carefully for any of the following bad habits:

1. Excessive or incorrect use of rudder during turns especially during patterns and rope breaks.
2. Poor airspeed control.
3. Not watching for other aircraft.
4. The need of full or no dive brakes on final approach or poor pattern planning.
5. Careless preflight, cockpit checklist or solo flight planning.
6. Low turns, undershooting or overshooting landings, stopping too close to other gliders or people.

Post-solo dual training will cover the following:

Steep turns
Crossed-control stalls
Spins
Spiral dives
Unassisted takeoffs (no wing runner)
Aero tow - low tow
Boxing the wake
Right hand landing patterns
Crosswind landings
Accuracy landings
Performance speeds
Cross country flight
Emergency procedures
Thermal, ridge, and wave soaring if possible
Exercising judgment

BADGES

In an effort to standardize flight-training programs, a series of badges has been established. These badges are administered by the Soaring Society of America, and are awarded by SSA instructors.

Requirements for the **A Badge** include:

PREFLIGHT PHASE
1. Sailplane nomenclature.
2. Sailplane handling procedures.
3. Sailplane preflight check.
4. Airport rules and FAR's.
5. Tow equipment signals and procedures.
6. Hook-up of tow rope or cable.
7. Takeoff signals.
8. Pilot responsibilities.

APPLICANT HOLDS:

1. Valid FAA student pilot certificate.
2. Suitable logbook.

PRE-SOLO PHASE:

Applicant has completed the following minimum flight-training program:

1. Familiarization flight.
2. Cockpit check procedure.
3. Effects of controls, on the ground and in flight.
4. Takeoff procedure, crosswind takeoffs.
5. Flight during tow.
6. Straight and level flight.
7. Simple turns.
8. Circuit procedure and landing patterns.
9. Landing procedure, downwind, crosswind landings.
10. Moderate and steep turns up to 720 degrees.
11. Stalls and stall recoveries.
12. Conditions of spin entry and spin recovery.
13. Effective use of spoilers/flaps and slips.
14. Emergency procedures.
15. Oral exam on FAR's.
16. Solo Flight.

Requirements for the **B Badge** are:

Demonstration of soaring ability by solo flight at least 30 minutes duration after release from a 2,000 foot tow. Add 1 1/2 minutes for each additional 100 ft. above 2,000 ft.

The **C Badge** is intended to recognize the pilot's potential ability for cross-country flight. The requirements for the C Badge are:

Pre-cross country phase.

1. Dual soaring practice, including instruction in techniques for soaring thermals, ridges and waves. (Simulated flight and/or ground instruction may be used when suitable conditions do not exist.)

2. Have knowledge of:
   a. Cross country procedures recommended in the America Soaring Handbook.
   b. Glider assembly, disassembly and retrieving.
   c. Dangers of cross country flying.

3. Solo practice. (Two hours minimum.)

4. Demonstrate soaring ability by a solo flight of at least 60 minutes duration after release from a 2,000 ft. (or lower) tow. (Add 1 1/2 minutes for each additional 100 ft. above 2,000 ft. tow.)

5. While accompanied by an SSA instructor, demonstrate ability to:
   a. Make a simulated off field landing approach, without reference to an altimeter.
   b. Perform an accuracy landing from the approach, touching down and coming to a complete stop within an area 500 ft. in length.

Note: The approach to the airport will begin at least one mile from the field and at an altitude sufficiently high to safely complete the maneuver and landing. The instructor will specify the boundaries of the landing area.

THE BRONZE BADGE

There was a gap in the training of glider pilots between the Soaring Society of America's ABC training program and the FAI Silver Badge. A new glider pilot with a "C" badge did not have the skills needed to make accurate off-field landings.

In 1982 I proposed a new Bronze badge to help close this knowledge gap. The Soaring Society of America adopted it in 1983.

The following are the requirements for the Bronze Badge:

1. Complete the ABC program with the C Badge awarded.

2. Log at least 15 solo hours in gliders, including 30 solo flights of which at least 10 are flown in a single place glider if possible.

3. Log at least two flights, each of which have two hours duration or more.

4. Perform at least three solo spot landings in a glider witnessed by an SSA instructor. The accuracy and distance parameters are based on the glider's performance, current winds, runway surface condition, and density altitude. As a guideline, a minimum distance of 400 feet would be acceptable for a Schweizer 2-33. (This is a land and stop in a specified zone requirement.)

5. Log dual time in gliders with an instructor during which at least two accuracy landings (same as above) were made without reference to an altimeter to simulate off-field and strange field landings. These landings should occur at a different airport if possible.

6. Pass a closed book written examination covering cross-country techniques and knowledge. Minimum passing grade is 80%.

It is important for you to complete the entire ABC badges, the Bronze Badge, the Silver Altitude requirement (1000 meter altitude gain) and the five hour Duration requirement before you consider flying cross country. Completing all of these requirements demonstrates you have developed the minimum flying skills and knowledge necessary to fly cross country. These awards have been developed to help develop your flying skills before you attempt any actual cross country flying.

The intention of the three accuracy landings as stated in item four is for these accuracy landings be three successful landings in a row, from three different patterns, left hand, right hand, and downwind. The downwind landing would be done with little or no wind. The two landings with an instructor in item five is performed at a strange site, such as another airport the student is not familiar with.

F.A.I. SOARING AWARDS

The Silver Badge, Gold Badge, and Gold badge with Diamonds are soaring awards granted to pilots for flights satisfying the qualifications of each badge as set forth in the sporting code of The Federation Aeronautique Internationale (FAI).

QUALIFICATIONS AND REQUIREMENTS

SILVER BADGE

Distance: a straight flight of at least 50 km (31.1 miles).

Duration: a flight of at least 5 hours.

Height: a gain in height of at least 1000 meters (3,281 feet).

The distance leg may also be an out to a pre-declared goal and return to the starting point or a triangle flight with one leg more than 50 km. A pre-flight declaration must be made and photographs taken.

GOLD BADGE

Distance: a flight of at least 300 kilometers (186.4 miles).

Duration: a flight of at least 5 hours.

Height: a gain in height of at least 3,000 meters (9,842 feet).

DIAMONDS

There are 3 diamonds:

Diamond Goal: a flight of at least 300 kilometers (186.4 miles) over a pre-declared triangular or an out and return course.

Diamond Distance: a flight of at least 500 kilometers (310.7 miles)

Diamond Height: a gain in height of at least 5,000 meters (16,404 feet).

1,000 KILOMETER BADGE

The FAI will award a special badge and diploma to pilots achieving a distance flight of at least 1,000 kilometers (621 miles).

146

THE SOARING SOCIETY OF AMERICA

The SSA is a nonprofit organization of enthusiasts who seek to foster and promote all phases of soaring flight. It supervises FAI related activities such as record attempts, competition sanctions, and the FAI badge program.

The journal of the Soaring Society is Soaring Magazine. This magazine is considered by many to be the preeminent of all soaring magazines.

You will want to join this organization by sending for membership forms at the following address:

SSA
PO Box 2100
Hobbs, New Mexico 88241

Phone (505) 392-1177
email: feedback@ssa.org

THE SOARING SOCIETY OF AMERICA

The SSA is a nonprofit organization of enthusiasts who seek to foster and promote all phases of soaring flight. It supervises FAI related activities such as record attempts, competition sanctions, and the FAI badge program.

The journal of the Soaring Society is Soaring Magazine. This magazine is considered by many to be the preeminent of all soaring magazines.

You will want to join this organization by sending for membership forms at the following address:

ANSWERS TO WRITTEN TEST #1

1. Nomenclature

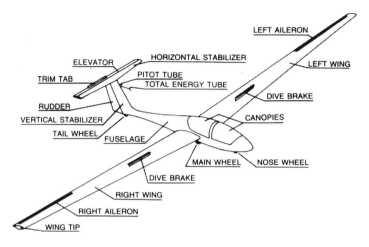

2. Why does an aircraft have?

a. Ailerons: to control angle of bank.

b. Elevator: to control angle of attack.

c. Rudder: to counteract aileron drag.

3. What does the wing do? Generates lift as air passes over and under it.

4. What is angle of attack? The angle the relative airflow meets an airfoil.

5. Name three things that happen when angle of attack is changed.

a. Lift capability changes.

b. Drag changes.

c. Speed changes.

6. Pushing on the left rudder pedal will cause the nose of the glider to yaw which way? Left.

7. Why does a glider have a yaw string? To show if the glider is flying streamlined.

8. In the following drawing, which rudder should be pressed to straighten the yaw string? The right rudder.

9. Before making a turn, a pilot should always look for other aircraft in the direction of the intended turn.

10. What turns an aircraft? Lift of the wing being tilted.

WRITTEN TEST #2 - STABILITY

1. Name the three axes of the glider.

a. Roll or longitudinal axis.

b. Pitch or lateral axis.

c. Yaw or vertical axis.

2. When the glider moves about any axis, it rotates about the center of gravity.

3. The glider fuselage tends to fly streamlined through the relative airflow because of the weathervane effect and thus is stable about the yaw (vertical) axis.

4. The glider tends to fly with its wings level because the wings are mounted on the fuselage at an angle called dihedral.

5. Pitch stability is achieved by a balancing act between the horizontal stabilizer, wing lift, and the center of gravity.

WRITTEN TEST #3 - SHALLOW, MEDIUM AND STEEP TURNS

1. When a pilot "flies" an aircraft, only three things are being controlled. They are:

a. Direction.

b. Speed.

c. Flying efficiently, or keeping the aircraft streamlined through the air.

2. In a shallow turn the pilot will need to hold some aileron into the turn because of the roll stability.

3. In a steep turn the pilot will need to hold some aileron against the turn because of the overbanking tendency.

4. During all turns, some rudder pressure will be needed in the direction of the turn.

WRITTEN TEST #4 - PREFLIGHT

1. What is meant by "popped" rivets?

A popped rivet is any loose rivet.

2. What would cause a popped rivet?

Overstressing the metal the rivets hold causes popped rivets.

3. What are some common signs of possible hidden damage?

Popped rivets, wrinkled skin, distorted hinges, bent dive brakes, dents.

4. What should you look for when checking the tow release mechanism? Cleanliness, spring tension, wear.

5. What would distorted hinges on the ailerons or dive brakes indicate? Stresses caused by mis-use above maneuvering or redline speed.

6. What should a student pilot do if evidence of damage or excessive wear is found? Report to the instructor or mechanic.

7. What documents are required in a glider?

Operating manual.

Airworthiness certificate.

Registration.

8. What should you look for when checking the pitot tube?

Cleanliness, obstructions, covers removed.

9. How can you insure that you check every important preflight item? Use a written checklist.

10. Who is responsible for checking the tow rope before each flight? The pilot of the glider.

150

WRITTEN TEST #5 - FORWARD STALLS

1. What is a stall? When an airfoil exceeds its critical angle of attack.

2. Name 6 signs of an impending stall in the order they occur.

> a. Excessive back stick pressure.
>
> b. Nose high attitude.
>
> c. Low airspeed.
>
> d. Quietness.
>
> e. Mushy controls.
>
> f. Buffeting.

3. Where on the wing does a stall first occur? Usually near the inboard trailing edge of the wing.

4. When the wing stalls, the glider pitches nose down. Why? Primarily because the center of gravity is located well forward of the center of pressure.

5. What is the minimum stalling speed of the glider you are being trained in?
2-33, 41 m.p.h. (36 knots)   Grob G 103, 41 knots

6. Can a glider stall at a higher airspeed? How?
Yes.
Increased weight.
Turns.
Forward CG loading.
Dirt, bugs, damage on wings.
Open dive brakes.
Turbulence.
Sloppy flying.

7. Why is it important to practice stalls?
So a pilot will recognize the impending stall early and make a quick, positive recovery with a minimum loss of altitude, with no tendency toward a "secondary" stall.

8. How is a normal recovery made from a forward stall?
a. Stick forward, get the nose of the glider below the horizon.
b. Pause until flying speed is regained.
c. Resume normal flight. Do not bring nose back up above horizon.

9. If a wing starts to "drop" during a forward stall, how should that wing be raised? Why?

With opposite rudder. Opposite aileron would cause an increased angle of attack on the wing that is already at, or near its critical angle of attack.

WRITTEN TEST #6 - TURNING STALLS

1. Turning stalls are most dangerous close to the ground. Why?

Because of the pilot's attempt to keep the aircraft up, by pulling back on the control stick. This is a natural reaction in a high stress situation. It can only be overcome with thorough training practice, and understanding how an aircraft works.

2. Name the three occasions turning stalls most likely to happen?

a. Turns in the landing pattern.

b. Low altitude thermalling.

c. Rope breaks.

3. A turning stall is most easily entered from a:

Shallow turn. Turning stalls entered from shallow turns often become spins. Without an abrupt elevator movement, most gliders cannot be made to stall or spin from steeper turns.

4. Give a step-by-step recovery procedure from a turning stall.

a. Opposite rudder.

b. Stick forward.

c. Pause, regain flying speed.

d. Roll level with ailerons and bring nose to normal attitude below the horizon.

5. How do you prevent turning stalls close to the ground?

Avoid low altitude turns by using proper planning.

Keep the nose below the horizon so the glider flies at a proper airspeed.

Use an adequate bank angle.

Keep the yaw string straight.

6. What is one control not to use during the first steps of a turning stall recovery?

Opposite aileron.

7. From the standpoint of turning stalls, the safest turn is a:

A steep turn.

WRITTEN TEST #7 - LANDINGS

1. What is the dive brake open glide ratio of most sailplanes? 5:1

2. What is the maximum glide ratio of the trainer you fly?

2-33 = about 20:1 actual.

Grob G 103 = about 32:1 actual

3. Below 1,000 feet AGL a pilot should never _____?

Circle, or turn away from the landing area.

4. What is the three-item pre landing checklist performed at the I.P.?

a. Hand on dive brake handle.

b. Disregard altimeter.

c. Establish pattern airspeed.

5. What is the primary judgmental decision to be made during the downwind leg? Where to turn into base leg.

6. What two checkpoints are used during the downwind leg?

Point "A" opposite the touch down point.

Point "B" at a 45-degree angle to the touch down point.

7. What is the normal sink rate during the downwind leg?

2 - 4 knots or 200 - 400 feet per minute.

8. What should you do if you experienced excessive sink during the downwind leg? Close dive brakes and turn into base leg earlier.

9. What would you do if you encountered lift during the downwind leg? Open dive brake and possibly extend downwind leg.

10. How should the turn into base leg be made?

Well banked.

Constant, appropriate airspeed.

Straight yaw string.

11. Upon completion of the turn into base leg, you realize that you are too high. What will you do?

Open dive brakes and possible make a slight turn away from the landing area.

12. You are on base leg ready to turn into final and realize you are too high. There is one type of pattern that should be avoided. What is it?

Button hook pattern.

13. On final it is important to maintain a constant airspeed using the elevator control, and "freeze" the desired touchdown point on the windshield using which control?

Dive brakes.

14. On final you realize that you are above the 5:1 glide slope. As a student pilot you should:

Open dive brakes and land further down the runway?

15. As an experienced pilot, when might you find the TLAR method most useful?

Off field and strange airport landings.

BASIC GLOSSARY OF AVIATION TERMINOLOGY

Aviation has a unique vocabulary all its own. You will find the following glossary to be helpful in understanding some of the terms you will hear at the gliderport.

Accelerated Stall. A stalled angle of attack of the wing at an airspeed above the minimum for that condition.

AGL Above Ground Level.

Aileron. A hinged control surface on the wing to aid in producing a banking or rolling movement about the longitudinal axis.

Aircraft. A device that is used or intended to be used for flight in the air.

Airfoil. Any member, or surface, on an airplane whose major function is to deflect the airflow. Primarily the wing and tail surfaces.

Airplane. An engine driven fixed wing aircraft heavier than air, that is supported in flight by the dynamic reaction of the air against its wings.

Airport Traffic Area. That airspace within a horizontal radius of 5 statute miles from the center of any airport at which a control tower is operating, extended from the surface up to, but not including 3,000 feet above the elevation of the airport.

Air Traffic Control (ATC.) A service operated by appropriate authority to promote the safe, orderly, and expeditious flow of air traffic.

Airworthy. The status of being in condition suitable for safe flight.

Altimeter. An instrument for indicating the relative altitude of an airplane by measuring atmospheric pressure.

Altitude. The elevation of an airplane. This can be specified as above sea level, or above the ground over which it flies.

Anemometer. A device for measuring the velocity of the wind.

Angle Of Attack. The acute angle measured between the chord line of an airfoil and the relative wind.

Angle of Incidence. The angle between the chord line of the wing and the longitudinal axis of the glider.

Aspect Ratio. The ratio between the span and the mean chord of the wings.

Attitude. The position of an aircraft considering the inclination of its axes in relation to the horizontal.

Axis. The theoretical line extending through the center of gravity in each major plane. The three axes are longitudinal, lateral, and vertical.

Bank. To tip or roll about the longitudinal axis of the aircraft.

Barograph. A recording barometer. It records altitude, and time. A recording of a flight is called a barogram.

Best Glide Speed. The airspeed that results in the flattest glide obtainable in calm air.

Buffeting. The beating effect of the disturbed air stream on an aircraft's structure during flight.

Calibrated Airspeed. Indicated airspeed of an aircraft, corrected for position and instrument error.

Ceiling (aircraft.) The maximum altitude an aircraft is capable of attaining.

Ceiling (meteorology.) The height of the base of the clouds above ground.

Center of Gravity. The point within an aircraft through which, for balance purposes, the total force of gravity is considered to act.

Checklist. A list, usually carried in the pilot's compartment, of items requiring the airman's attention for various flight operations.

Checkpoint. A prominent landmark on the ground which is used to establish the position of an aircraft in flight.

Chord. The width of an airfoil.

Controlled Airspace. Air space means airspace of defined dimensions within which air traffic control service is provided to IFR flights and to VFR flights in accordance with the airspace classification. Generically considered to be Class A, Class B, Class C, Class D, and Class E airspace.

Convection. The up or down movement of the air due to thermal action.

Coordination. The movement or use of two or more controls in their proper relationship to obtain the desired results.

Crossed Controls. Application of left rudder and right aileron simultaneously or vice versa.

Cumulonimbus Cloud (CuNim.) Clouds with great vertical development, often with tower-like summits, and anvil-shaped tops. Very dangerous.
Cumulus Clouds. Single clouds with some vertical thickness. Indicates good soaring conditions.

Deviation. The error induced in a magnetic compass by steel structure, electrical equipment, and similar disturbing factors in the aircraft.

Dive Brakes. Drag producing panels on the wings that are primarily used for glide path control.

Drag Force. opposing the motion of the aircraft through the air.

Drogue Chute. A deployable small parachute attached to the tail of a sailplane which when deployed, increases drag to permit steeper landing approaches and shorter landing rollouts.

Elevator. A hinged, horizontal control surface used to control the angle of attack of the wing, by changing the pitch attitude.

Empennage. The entire tail group of an aircraft, including the fixed and movable tail surfaces.

Fairing. A member or structure the primary function of which is to produce a smooth outline and reduce drag.

Federal Aviation Agency (FAA.) The governing body of civil aviation in the U.S.A.

Federation Aeronautique Internationale (FAI.) The world governing body of aeronautical contests and custodian of world records.

Flap. An appendage to the wing for changing its airfoil shape and lift characteristics to permit slower landings and improved performance at high speeds.

Flare Out. To "round out" for the touch down (landing) by decreasing the rate of descent and airspeed by slowly raising the nose.

Flight Plan. A detailed outline of a proposed flight filed with a flight service station before a cross-country flight.

Fuselage. The body to which the wings, and tail are attached.

'G.' The load on the glider's structure as stated in terms of multiples of the force of gravity. A 3G load would be three times the load applied by gravity alone.

Glide. Sustained forward flight in which speed is maintained by the loss of altitude.

Glider A heavier-than-air aircraft, that is supported in flight by the dynamic reaction of the air against its lifting surfaces and whose free flight does not depend primarily on an engine.

Glide Ratio. The ratio of forward to downward motion, numerically the same as the ratio of lift to drag, L/D.

Ground Effect. The temporary gain in lift during flight at very low altitudes due to the compression of the air between the wings of an aircraft and the ground.

Ground Loop. An uncontrollable violent turn on the ground.

Ground Speed. The speed with reference to the earth.

Heading. The direction the aircraft is pointed.

High Tow. During aero tow, the position slightly above the tow plane's wake.

IFR Conditions. Weather conditions below the minimum for flight under visual flight rules.

Incidence, Angle Of. The angle between the mean chord of the wing and the longitudinal axis of the aircraft.

Indicated Airspeed. The speed of an aircraft as shown on its pitot static airspeed indicator.

Induced Drag. Drag force created by the production of lift. Decreasing airspeed increases induced drag.

Knot. A unit of speed equaling one nautical mile per hour. One nautical mile equals 6080 feet.

L/D. Lift divided by drag. Numerically the same as glide ratio.

Leading Edge. The forward edge of any airfoil.

Lenticular Cloud. Lens-shaped cloud formed by mountain wave or lee wave.

Load Factor. The sum of the loads on a structure, expressed in ' G' units.

Longeron. The principal longitudinal structural member in a fuselage.

Low Tow. In aero tow, the position of the glider when it is slightly below the wake of the tow plane.

Macready Speed Ring. A moveable ring around a variometer that shows speeds to fly for various rates of climb or descent.

Maintenance. Means inspection, overhaul, repair, preservation, and the replacement of parts, but excludes preventive maintenance.

Maneuvering Speed. Maximum speed at which the flight controls can be fully deflected without damage to the aircraft structure.

Minimum Controllable Airspeed. That airspeed, just above the stall, where any reduction of airspeed would result in indications of a stall.

Minimum Sink Speed. The airspeed at which the aircraft loses altitude most slowly.

Netto. A device that allows the variometer to show only the vertical movement of the airmass surrounding the glider.

Night. The time between the end of evening civil twilight and the beginning of morning civil twilight, as published in the American Air Almanac, converted to local time.

Open-Class Sailplanes. Gliders with no restrictions as to size or aerodynamic devices.

Overbanking Tendency. In a turn, the effect of the outer wing going faster than the inner wing and thus producing more lift, which steepens the bank.

Overdevelopment. An increase in cloud cover to the extent that the sun's radiational heating is reduced, thus reducing or even stopping thermal activity.

Overshoot. To fly beyond a designated area or mark.

Parachute. A device used to retard the fall of a person or object through the air.

Parasitic Drag. Drag produced by the aircraft's passage through the air. Increases with airspeed.

Penetrate. The ability to progress through the resistance of the air.

Pilot. One who operates the controls of an aircraft in flight.

Pilotage. Navigation by visual reference to landmarks.

Pilot In Command. The pilot responsible for the operation and safety of an aircraft during flight time.

Pitch Attitude. The angle of the longitudinal axis of the aircraft to the horizon. (Nose high or Low.)

Pitot Tube. A tube exposed to the air stream for measuring impact air pressure.

Placard. A required statement of operation limitations that is permanently affixed where it can be seen by the pilot in flight.

Porpoising. Repeated pitching (up and down) of an aircraft.

Preventive Maintenance. Simple or minor preservation operations and the replacement of small standard parts not involving complex operations.

Prohibited Area. Designated airspace within which the flight of aircraft is prohibited.

Red Line. Maximum airspeed marked by a red line on the airspeed indicator.

Registration Certificate. Statement of ownership and identifying numbers of an aircraft.

Relative Wind. The direction of an airflow with respect to an airfoil.

Roll. Displacement around the longitudinal axis of an aircraft.

Rotor. Swirling air circulation under the crest of a mountain wave. This is an area of severe turbulence.

Rudder. Hinged vertical control surface used primarily to induce or overcome yawing moments about the vertical axis.

Rudder Pedals. Controls within the aircraft by means of which the rudder is actuated.

Sailplane. A glider whose performance is high enough to permit soaring flight.

Sea Breeze Front. Zone of convergence between cool air over a body of water and warm inland air.

Sequence Report. The weather report transmitted hourly to all teletype stations, and available at all Flight Service Stations.

Sink. Descending air currents that cause a sailplane to lose altitude more rapidly than calm air.

Skid. Sideward motion of an aircraft in flight produced by centrifugal force and too much rudder in turns.

Slip. Sideways motion of an aircraft toward the lowered wing.

Slipstream. The current of air driven by the propeller.

Soar. To fly without artificial power and without loss of altitude.

Soaring Society of America (SSA.) Delegated governing body for all soaring activities in the U.S.A.

Solo. A flight during which a pilot is the only occupant of the aircraft.

Span.. The maximum distance from wing tip to wing tip of an aircraft.

Spar The principal longitudinal structural member of an airfoil.

Speed-To-Fly. The indicated airspeed which produces the flattest glide in any given airmass.

Spin. A prolonged stall in which an aircraft rotates about its center of gravity while it descends, usually with its nose well down.

Spoilers. Devices that primarily disturb the airflow over the wing and to "spoil" part of the lift, resulting in a steeper glide path.

Stability. The tendency of an aircraft in flight to remain in straight, level, upright flight, or to return to this attitude if displaced, without attention of the pilot.

Stabilizer. The fixed airfoil of an aircraft used to increase stability; usually the aft fixed horizontal surface to which the elevator is hinged (horizontal stabilizer).

Stable Air. An air mass in which there is little or no vertical air movement.

Stall. The abrupt loss of a considerable part of the lift when the angle of attack increases to a point at which the flow of air tends to break away from a wing or other airfoil.

Static Port. A source of air on a sailplane that is unaffected by dynamic forces.

Terminal Forecasts. Weather forecasts available each six hours at all Flight Service Stations.

Terminal Velocity. The theoretical maximum speed which could be obtained in a dive.

Thermal. Usually a rising column of air that is warmer than the surrounding air at ambient temperature.

Total Energy Variometer. A variometer compensated with a device to show only changes in the actual climb or descent of the sailplane; thus a change in airspeed due to stick deflections will not register as lift of sink on the variometer.

Traffic Pattern. The traffic flow that is prescribed for aircraft landing at, taxiing on, or taking off from an airport.

True Airspeed. The actual airspeed of an aircraft relative to undisturbed air.

Variometer. A sensitive instrument that indicates rate of climb or descent.

Visibility. The greatest horizontal distance which prominent objects on the ground can be seen.

VFR Conditions. Weather conditions above the minimum for flight under visual flight rules.

Weak Link. A short section of rope or other device that meets the strength requirements (specified by the FAA) that is incorporated when stronger tow ropes and cables are used.

Weathervane. The tendency of an aircraft to face into the relative wind due to its effect on the vertical surfaces of the tail group.

Wind Gradient. The decrease in wind speed close to the ground due to the frictional effect of the terrain, buildings, trees, etc.

Wind Shift. An abrupt change in the direction or velocity or both, of the wind.

Wind Sock. A cloth sleeve, mounted aloft at an airport to use in estimating wind direction and speed.

Wing. An airfoil whose major function is to provide lift by the dynamic reaction to the mass of air swept downward.

Wing Root. The end of a wing which joins the fuselage.

Wing Tip. The end of the wing farthest from the fuselage.

Yaw. To rotate about the vertical axis.

Books you should have in your library:

The following are suggested texts to help you develop a small reference library:

Accident Prevention Manual by Thomas Knauff

After Solo by Thomas Knauff

Aviation Weather, AC 00-6A, (Government Publication)

FAR's For Glider Pilots by Doris Grove

Federal Aviation Regulations, part 1, 43, 61, 91, 830 (Government Publication)

Glider Basics From First Flight To Solo by Thomas Knauff

Glider flight manual by manufacturer of glider

Glider Flying Handbook, FAA-H-8083-13 (Government Publication)

Pilot's Handbook of Aeronautical Knowledge, FAA-H-8083-25 (Government Publication)

Other Recommended books:

Stick and Rudder by Wolfgang Langewiesche.

Knauff & Grove Soaring Supplies
3523 South Eagle Valley Road
Julian, Pa 16844

Phone (814) 355 2483
FAX (814) 355 2633

www.eglider.org

Continuing Education.

This is your first flight training manual. There is no reason to rush out and buy a lot of books, however, when you near the completion of your pre-solo flight training, you should have read *Accident Prevention Manual For Glider Pilots*, and purchase *After Solo* by Tom Knauff.

After Solo has all the flight training requirements to complete your private glider license. It includes many advanced soaring techniques, and an important chapter on emergency procedures. Other text books will be necessary and the short list is included on the previous page.

The Cost of Flying Gliders

Learning to fly gliders is relatively expensive. You must pay for the instructor, the glider, the tow plane and the tow pilot, making each flight more expensive than renting a power plane for a flying lesson.

That's the bad news. The good news is after you learn to fly and have your glider license, the costs of gliding can be very inexpensive. A share of a glider can be only a few thousand dollars. One four member partnership at our gliderport owns a beautiful Schleicher Ka-6. Each partner paid $1,500 for their share.

Maintenance costs are minimal with the most expensive being the required annual inspection (about $150.) If they choose to keep the glider assembled in a hanger, each partner pays $15 per month. Insurance adds about $10 per month for each partner.

For the price of an aerotow, they can fly all day long assuming they choose a day with a reasonable good chance of soarable lift.

Some years from now, when they choose to sell their glider, they almost certainly will be able to recoop their initial expense.

Few activities allow a person to have the extraordinary experiences and fellowship the sport of soaring offers for such a low cost.

Even a modern, high performance fiberglass sailplane can be purchased used for a fraction of the price of a new one. Since we only fly a relatively few hours each year, partnerships make good economical sense. Be sure to buy a popular, name brand glider and you will be sure to sell it years later for what you paid.

Index

A

accidental stall 75
adverse yaw 21
aerotow 63
aileron 13, 16, 17, 77, 83
aileron drag 21, 26, 39, 66
airfoil 7
airspeed 10
airspeed indicator 4, 52
airworthiness certificate 51
altimeter 3
angle of attack
    9, 14, 35, 48, 69, 77, 78, 83
angle of bank 39, 40
angle of incidence 35
attitude 72
audio 6
axes 31

B

bank 34
bank angle 19, 26
barometric pressure 3

C

C.G. 31
canopy 50, 68
capacity 5
center of gravity 13, 14, 31, 35, 71
center of lift 35
center of pressure 35
centrifugal force 48
clearing the turn 39
clearing turns 41
cockpit checklist 39, 43
control stick 13, 14, 25, 26
coordinated turn 22
coordination 39
critically slow airspeeds 83
crosswind 58
crosswind takeoff 59

D

dihedral 34
dive brake 13, 68
drag 10

E

elevator 13, 14, 50, 79
emergencies 84

F

F.A.A. 51
falling 79
flaps 13, 68
flight computer 6
flight manual 51
forward stall recovery 71

G

glide ratio 7
glider 1
gravity 8
ground loop 68

H

horizon 14, 23, 26, 39, 71, 83
horizontal stabilizer 14, 35

I

imminent stalls 75
indicated airspeed 70
instinctive reactions 83

L

lateral axis 32
leading edge 35
lift 7, 9, 15
lift distribution curve 35
line inspection 51
longitudinal axis 32

O

opposite rudder 75
overbanking tendency 45

P

pilot induced oscillations 58
pitch 14, 32
pitch attitude 14, 23, 26, 39, 75
pitch stability 35
pitot 4
popped rivets 52
positive control check 53
preflight checklist 53
preflight inspection 51
primary flight controls. 13
propwash 59, 63

R

rate of turn 19
reduced G sensation 74
Registration Certificate 51
relative airflow 8, 17, 34, 36
relative wind 8
release knob 59
release mechanism 67
roll 32
roll rate 26
roll stability 34, 45
rotational force 35
rudder 13, 20
rudder pedals 27
rudder waggle 57
running the wing 67

S

sailplane 1
seat belts 52
sideslip 34
sink rate 7
six signs of a stall 71
six signs of the stall 75
speed-to-fly ring 6
spin 83

spoilers 13
stall 69
static vent 3
steps of a turn 40
stick thermals 5
stress 84

T

tail 14
thermistors 5
total energy 5
total energy probe 5
tow position 63
tow ring 67
tow rope 67
trailing edge 35, 72
trim 25, 39
turbulence 79
turn 18
turning stall 77
twist 72

V

variometer 5, 52
vertical axis 31

W

wake 64
walk around inspection 53
weathervane 33, 60
weight and balance 53
Wilber Wright 24
wind gradient 79
wind shear 79
windsock 57
wing 7
wing loading 84
wing runner 57

Y

yaw 31, 73, 77, 83
yaw stability 33, 36, 79
yaw string 24, 27, 39, 84

Pierce Brosnan, & Rene Russo filming "The Thomas Crown Affair" in Schempp-Hirth Duo Discus.